Global Flashpoints 2015

Global Flashpoints 2015
Crisis and Opportunity

Editors
Craig Cohen
Josiane Gabel

CSIS | CENTER FOR STRATEGIC &
INTERNATIONAL STUDIES

ROWMAN & LITTLEFIELD
Lanham • Boulder • New York • London

Center for Strategic & International Studies
1616 Rhode Island Avenue, NW
Washington, DC 20036
2002-887-0200 | www.csis.org

Published by Rowman & Littlefield
A wholly owned subsidiary of
The Rowman & Littlefield Publishing Group, Inc.
4501 Forbes Boulevard, Suite 200, Lanham, Maryland 20706
www.rowman.com

Unit A, Whitacre Mews, 26-34 Stannary Street, London SE11 4AB

Library of Congress Control Number: 2015930349

ISBN: 978-1-4422-4629-4 (cloth)
ISBN: 978-1-4422-4630-0 (pbk)
ISBN: 978-1-4422-4631-7 (electronic)

Contents

INTRODUCTION
Is America in Retreat?

John J. Hamre

As the 2016 presidential election race begins, both parties look schizophrenic on foreign and defense policy. Three factors create this wavering between isolationist and internationalist visions: budgets, who gets to wear the mantle of "strong on defense," and the horizontal nature of the problems we face. The result is a policy debate that doesn't conform to traditional battle lines. This has left the rest of the world wondering two things. Is America in retreat? And will the upcoming election settle this question or prolong it?

Let me start with the politics of defense budgets. There is an internal political dynamic in Washington for defense budgets that is only indirectly related to the threats the country faces. Over the past 30 years, one of the dominant factors in budget politics has been a Republican Party that maintains "strong defense" as an essential component of its ideological base. Democrats were traumatized by the Vietnam War, and so despite a few notable exceptions, they were deeply ambivalent about defense over this period.

Over the past six years, however, Democrats were able to emerge from the shadow of Vietnam. They were able to portray the party as sensible on national security after the overreach of the Bush administration on Iraq. The courageous strike on Osama bin Laden, the hated mastermind of the attack on 9/11, further shielded Democrats to the charge that they were soft on defense. But this also meant that there was no longer a great electoral benefit to Republicans to being defense champions.

This trend coincided with the emergence of the Tea Party as the energetic base of the Republican Party. Tea Party conservatives came to Washington believing that the greatest national security risk we face is unbridled deficits. Former Vice President Dick Cheney famously said that deficits don't matter politically, but the Tea Party argued successfully that even Defense should be cut if that is how we need to get our national house in order. This sentiment still has a firm lock on Republicans, dividing them internally and blocking a consensus on defense spending. Democrats want to see greater domestic spending and are willing to increase defense to get it, but don't want to be seen as flagrant deficit spenders.

This is the dynamic that produced the sequester—the mindless, automatic process that cuts the federal budget by a set percentage unless Congress acts to replace it with another budget. Defense budgets have remained caught in this cycle in which discretionary spending—which will account for less than a third of federal spending in FY 2015—must shoulder the entire burden of reducing the deficit because Congress can't reach consensus on cutting entitlements or raising taxes. Stepping out of this cycle will require positive action from both parties to compromise, a lost art in Washington these days.

The result of this domestic political dynamic is that neither party has established a consensus for a sustained commitment abroad. In fact, both parties have strong wings questioning our existing commitments. These isolationist arguments resonate with Americans after 12 years of war. But the challenges we face internationally do not lend themselves to quick fixes or retreating behind Fortress America. Let me use the example of the two external crises commanding our attention at present—Ebola and the Islamic State of Iraq and Syria (ISIS).

Now that the Ebola virus has spread to the United States, we have become alert as a nation to a problem that we thought was limited to Africa. At the same time the news is deeply troubling in Iraq that ISIS continues its march across the desert, expanding its demonic remit.

These two crises seem quite unconnected, yet they share fundamental qualities. Ebola has erupted periodically in Africa for at least decades. It always remained contained in its local setting, gradually disappearing back into the natural environment into what epidemiologists call the "reservoir" where it remains until the next outbreak.

We have had terrorists for over a millennium in the Middle East. But historically those terrorists had only parochial aspirations. Now we have a virulent ISIS that threatens Europe and America via repugnant videos released on the Internet.

While these are different forms of pestilence, they both become global concerns because of two factors. The first is the ease of movement in the 21st century—the movement of people, information, ideas, disease, and commercial goods. The second half of the 20th century saw a revolution in commerce and technology. American consumers depend on distant factories that transport goods in container ships within short weeks. Millions of people a day are flying across the globe. Technology has sped the transit of people, goods, and disease at unprecedented speed. In one sense it is amazing it took four months before Ebola showed up in America.

The second factor that underlies ISIS and Ebola is that both exploded in areas with weak governments and poor infrastructure. Corruption undercuts the legitimacy and effectiveness of governments. The void is a breeding ground for all forms of pestilence.

Both ISIS and Ebola have caused deep anxieties here in Washington. I hear politicians saying that we should shut down all air transportation from West Africa, for example. Until ISIS exploded in Syria and Iraq, the prevailing public sentiment was to walk away from Iraq and not get involved in Syria. Our fatigue with 12 years of war understandably caused Americans to simply want out of the whole mess.

But we all greatly benefit from this new global economy. Our prosperity and way of life are now inextricably connected into this global system. We can't simply quarantine our country from the rest of the world to avoid ISIS or Ebola or anything else. It was clear to health professionals six months ago that Ebola would come to America if we didn't mount a Marshall Plan-type effort to stop it in West Africa. It was clear three years ago the chaos in Syria would erupt into violent energy throughout the Middle East. We just didn't do anything.

President Obama was widely criticized at the time of the Libya invasion when the administration said it would "lead from behind." I thought the administration's position was wrong at the time. But I would reformulate that statement to capture what I think has to be our strategy to deal with ISIS, Ebola, and most modern threats: we have to lead from within.

We are not going to defeat ISIS with airplanes. We will have to be on the ground. But we will be on the ground in the middle of a coalition, predominantly made up of moderate Sunnis from Iraq and partner countries in the region. America has to be in the middle of it. We finally sent 3,000 military personnel to West Africa to provide logistics support for the health professionals there, who are struggling to contain Ebola at the source. Again, we have to be leading from within.

The question is whether our domestic politics can sustain the type of lasting effort required to lead from within. This is the overarching question that lies behind the articles in this annual CSIS publication. Is America's power of deterrence still credible? Can we sustain our alliances and commitments abroad? Can we still shape events in places where our credibility has suffered? Will the world still look to us for political, security, and economic leadership, or are we seeing alternatives emerge?

In this modern era, there are very few unilateral actions America can take to solve the problems we face. Acting in concert with others doesn't mean America is leading from behind or is in retreat. Quite the opposite. We must build partnerships with those who need our help but lack the ability to solve problems on their own. I suspect that both parties' nominees for the presidency in 2016 will understand this. Americans are a pragmatic people. We adapt to the challenges we face.

The risk is that before this occurs, our domestic politics will evolve into a crisis of confidence in government. We now need, all the more, a bipartisan consensus. No enduring U.S. policy can be achieved without it.

I believe the world wants and needs U.S. leadership. We remain uniquely capable. The only thing that could truly send America into retreat is ourselves.

PART I

What Role Will Deterrence Play in America's National Security Strategy?

1. THE CASE FOR DETERRENCE

Kathleen H. Hicks

After a difficult year in U.S. foreign policy, some are wondering if the concept of deterrence still holds. Deterrence, though ancient in its basic precepts, came to prominence during the nuclear age when the United States was focused on convincing the Soviet Union that the costs and risks of direct military conflict would outweigh its potential benefits. With the dynamics of bipolar nuclear competition having long given way to a broader set of national security challenges, the U.S. government has made an effort to update its deterrence policy. Following the attacks of September 11, 2011, the U.S. government began to refer to "tailored deterrence," wherein the United States would tailor its approach to affecting the decision calculus of different potential adversaries in different circumstances.

Some argue that tailored deterrence has gone too far—that deterrence has become so context-specific and ubiquitous that it is no longer useful as an organizing principle of U.S. policy. These critics can point to documents like the 2010 National Security Strategy, in which the Obama administration made 17 references to deterrence, ranging from deterring armed conflict and aggression to deterring cyber intrusions and unlawful entry to the United States to deterring attacks on the international financial system. If deterrence has so many variations, can the United States effectively build policy around it?

The broad applicability of deterrence should not be seen as one of its failings. Deterrence was a key feature of foreign policy long before it carried the label and became synonymous with averting crises in strategic nuclear competition. Variations in the context for deterrence do, however, put a premium on effectively communicating to potential adversaries the risk-reward calculus they face in a particular circumstance. Communicating deterrent threats today is further complicated because norms are not yet firm in some domains of conflict, such as cyberspace, nor universally shared among key actors, such as in maritime disputes. Moreover, in an age of instant global communications and in which many deterrent contexts are present simultaneously, "tailored deterrence" can be difficult to execute, as key actors conflate word and deed in one case (usually U.S. inaction) with another.

The most damning critique of deterrence is far simpler: the concept is no longer useful because it does not work. Skeptics holding this view can point to incidents such as Russia's 2008 incursion into Georgia and 2014 annexation of Crimea, the recent rise of ISIS in defiance of international condemnation, repeated North Korean nuclear tests in the face of sanctions, and the Syrian regime's use of chemical weapons despite President Obama's "red line" as evidence that the United States does not have the credibility to deter threats. These incidents have taken place in the face of overwhelming U.S. military capability, the wielding of "exquisite" economic sanctions, and seemingly tireless diplomatic efforts (how many hours has Secretary of State Kerry been airborne these past 12 months?). If the United States, with all its current advantages, cannot deter others from undertaking actions it opposes, who can?

It is the United States itself that offers the most compelling case for the continuing relevance of deterrence: we are routinely deterred because we do not wish to risk the consequences—usually in blood and treasure—that taking certain actions might bring. And the United States in turn can deter well, especially against potentially catastrophic activity. U.S. nuclear capability and overwhelming conventional military power have forced many would-be rivals and non-state actors to pursue action in less deadly spheres, where it is difficult for the United States to bring these same advantages to bear.

The problem, then, is not with the concept of deterrence but rather its successful application. Our failures stem from three important shortcomings: in clarifying our interests, to ourselves and to others; in convincing others of our credibility in threatening those who challenge our interests; and in demonstrating the will and capability to fulfill those threats if deterrence fails. Moreover, U.S. credibility is more elastic than our leaders might like—the more deterrence fails or appears to fail in a particular context, the less credible U.S. threats are in that context, and often in other spheres. The good news is that leaders can often increase their credibility relatively quickly, as the administration has done this year by stepping-up its military capabilities along NATO's eastern border following Russia's annexation of Crimea.

It is time to set aside tired theoretical debates about deterrence to focus on concrete applications that fit today's dynamic environment. In the coming year, deterrence will be an aspect of virtually all our security dealings. From continuing nuclear challenges, to the conventional military sphere, to cyber and "cross-domain" challenges, to counterterrorism, deterrence will succeed only where American leaders can convince others that their actions (or inactions) risk greater costs than rewards. The results will usually be far less than desired: competition of interests will continue, and in some cases, the United States will care less about the outcome than those with opposing goals. This was true in the Cold War, from the creation of the Warsaw Pact to the Prague Spring, to, eventually, Vietnam, just as it was in 2014.

In 2015, the United States will need to build on its strong record of deterring existential threats to better deter those who threaten us short of war. Better application of deterrence requires clearly communicating what we care about and our willingness and capability to act in defense of those interests. Importantly, it also requires us to carry out threats when deterrence fails. Credibility can be gained just as it can be lost, but absent the wherewithal to carry out the deterrent threats we make—whether codified in our longstanding treaty commitments or simply stated by the president—more and potentially greater challenges to our interests will follow.

2. REBUILDING CREDIBILITY: REGIONAL PERSPECTIVES

A Conversation with Jon B. Alterman, Heather A. Conley, and Michael J. Green moderated by Stephanie Sanok Kostro

New realities within the international security environment—such as emerging threats from non-state adversaries—are causing U.S. officials to reevaluate how to use deterrence as a critical element of the nation's defense strategy. Senior Fellow Stephanie Sanok Kostro sat down with Senior Vice President, Zbigniew Brzezinski Chair in Global Security and Geostrategy, and Middle East Director Jon B. Alterman, Senior Vice President for Europe, Eurasia, and the Arctic and Europe Director Heather A. Conley, and Senior Vice President for Asia and Japan Chair Michael J. Green to discuss regional perceptions and opportunities for improved U.S. deterrence.

Stephanie Sanok Kostro: How do governments in your region of study perceive the current U.S. approach to deterrence?

Heather A. Conley: U.S. deterrence in Europe is expressed through NATO's Article 5 commitment that "an armed attack against one or more [ally] shall be considered an attack against them all." In addition, any ally can convene Article 4 consultations when it feels threatened. There have been only four post–Cold War instances of such consultations: three invoked by Turkey over Iraq/Syria and one by Poland over the Ukraine crisis. Invocation of these articles sends strong messages to the world about NATO—to include American—security concerns.

Michael J. Green: Although U.S. deterrence has long underwritten Asian security, there are serious questions in Asian capitals about U.S. deterrence. Many states worry about China's growing military capabilities and its assertive actions in territorial disputes. Japan and South Korea also focus on North Korea's largely unimpeded uranium and plutonium weapons programs. Simultaneously, chaos in Syria, Iraq, and Ukraine (as well as political dysfunction in Washington) elicits concern that the United States might "pivot" away from Asia or lack the willpower or resources to manage new security challenges.

Jon B. Alterman: There is a broad sense that U.S. deterrence is now less compelling, in part because of the Obama administration's perceived reluctance to use tools of influence and in part because of the Bush administration's inability to accomplish ambitious goals in the Middle East. While the region is fractured in many ways, there is virtual unanimity on one point: the Obama administration does not recognize pure evil when it sees it.

Also, the United States is trying to deter both Middle East state and non-state actors. States have assets to hold at risk, and rewards can be conferred. Non-state actors require a different set of tools and offer a different set of potential outcomes. U.S. tools are much better developed for the former.

Kostro: What are recent examples of successful U.S. deterrence efforts?

Alterman: While one might argue the United States is successfully deterring Iran from producing a nuclear weapon, the United States and its partners have failed to persuade Iran to end its nuclear program. Whether the current violence in the Middle

East represents the failure or success in U.S. deterrence efforts is unclear. The answer is probably a little of both.

Conley: Article 5 in some allies' minds equates to U.S. "boots on the ground." This is true in Poland and the Baltic states, which have lingering doubts whether some European countries would come to their aid if Russia invades. The most successful example was the recent deployment of 600 U.S. soldiers to the Baltic region and augmentation of U.S. forces in Poland following Russia's annexation of Crimea. It is also helpful that allies provided additional aircraft to NATO's Baltic air policing and based NATO's Multinational Corps-Northeast in Szczecin, Poland. Simply put, rhetoric is great, boots are required.

Green: The most obvious historical examples are deterrence of North Korea crossing the 38th Parallel and China crossing the Taiwan Strait. Today, some of the most difficult challenges are "gray zones," rather than black and white threats of invasion. China's pressure on its neighbors in the East and South China Seas presents a serious challenge for many in the region. Despite the U.S. rebalance to Asia, U.S. policymakers do not appear to have a clear strategy for deterring such "gray zone" conflicts, and Asian states will find it difficult to deter revision of the status quo on their own. There have been successes in reassuring allies about deterrence, including new dialogues with Japan and Korea and visible deployments of tactical aircraft and nuclear-capable bombers after threatening moves by North Korea.

Kostro: How could the United States improve deterrence activities?

Conley: The United States and NATO must meet the challenge of modern deterrence, and they must rapidly adapt, including developing the tools to confront Russia's unconventional means to influence the battle space, such as energy restrictions or support for anti-Europe parties. NATO must also be able to focus on its east and southeast flanks, given growing concern that concurrent tests of American and European policies in Ukraine and Syria will fail.

Alterman: The United States needs to be clearer about its interests, more willing to take action to further its interests, and more effective in creating consequences it seeks to create. Allies and adversaries alike judge that the United States is so inwardly focused and wary of Middle Eastern entanglements that they can safely predict the limits of U.S. action.

Green: I agree. Clarity and consistency in U.S. declarations will be critical. Washington's discourse has left Asian experts confused about the core strategic assumptions that animate U.S. policy. Do U.S. policymakers seek a balance of power centered on U.S. allies? Or a concert of power centered on Beijing? Or a combination of both that depends on which official is speaking and what is happening in the world? U.S. allies, partners, and adversaries are watching U.S. statements and actions. They will respond accordingly.

3. WHY DETERRENCE FAILED TO PREVENT SYRIAN USE OF WMD

Sharon Squassoni

When it comes to weapons of mass destruction (WMD) proliferation, it's hard not to like deterrence as a concept: it's much better to forestall WMD development than react to a fait accompli. Yet deterrence of WMD development and use is not simple. The Assad regime's use of chemical weapons against Syrian civilians in 2012 and 2013 is widely considered a failure of deterrence. The lessons of Syria are not easy, clear, or likeable for those contemplating future efforts to deter WMD proliferation.

From the beginning of the Syrian crisis, the Assad regime attempted to use the threat of WMD as a deterrent to external intervention. In July 2012, a foreign ministry spokesman claimed that, "Any stock of WMD or unconventional weapons that the Syrian Army possesses will never, never be used against the Syrian people or civilians during this crisis. . . . These weapons are made to be used strictly and only in the event of external aggression against the Syrian Arab Republic." President Obama's declaration of a red line the following month was probably not the response Assad had hoped for:

> We cannot have a situation where chemical or biological weapons are falling into the hands of the wrong people. We have been very clear to the Assad regime, but also to other players on the ground, that a red line for us is

we start seeing . . . chemical weapons moving around or being utilized. That would change my calculus.

Syrian chemical weapons subsequently killed 1,000 people in 2012 and 2013, but no direct foreign military interventions ensued. Instead, Assad used his chemical weapons stockpile as a bargaining chip against military intervention. By 2013, the international community (particularly Russia) succeeded in pressuring Syria to join the Chemical Weapons Convention and destroy its entire chemical arsenal. U.S. government officials have suggested that Russia and Syria thought the threat of U.S. military force was credible, but there is no way of knowing for sure. It was ultimately public outrage over the execution of American journalists and others by ISIS, not Syrian chemical weapons use, that prompted the U.S. military intervention in Syria in September 2014.

As the Syria case demonstrates, there are limits to deterring WMD proliferation. Knowing that Assad already had chemical weapons, President Obama's red line was aimed at their use or transfer to terrorists. However, use against Syrian civilians did not threaten U.S. vital interests, and it is hard to verify WMD transfer to terrorists. On Syria's nuclear capability, it is unlikely that deterrence was ever seriously considered by Israel, which covertly bombed the Al Kibar reactor in 2007. For Israel, Assad's construction of a nuclear reactor at Al Kibar threatened Israel's vital interests in a way that Syrian chemical weapons did not. Israel preemptively struck the reactor, the consequences of which have not entirely unfolded. (The bombing of the Osirak reactor prompted Iraq to embark on a massive nuclear program, which Assad is likely not to pursue.)

On a fundamental level, the clear signals and identifiable outcomes that define successful deterrence are tough to establish for WMD proliferation. Deterring WMD use may be easier than deterring WMD development, if only because WMD use is a clearly defined action (mostly), whereas WMD development is a process, and a deeply clandestine one at that. The challenges are further compounded when onward proliferation to terrorist groups (whether intentional or accidental) is added to the mix. In contrast, as long as WMD are thought to deter military action against a regime, they will be highly valued by proliferators, making WMD programs a vital interest. At the very least, giving up weapons or a program can buy time for a regime.

As a policy tool, then, deterrence is unwieldy in the nonproliferation world. It shares an uncomfortable bed with the treaties (such as the Non-Proliferation Treaty, Biological Weapons Convention, and Chemical Weapons Convention) that seek procedural responses to noncompliance and with the informal supplier arrangements that rely on cooperation to keep the most sensitive materials and equipment out of the hands of would-be proliferators. A decreasing number of countries stand outside these regimes, and for these, deterrence is most likely to be directed against use of WMD, or their transfer to terrorist groups.

Despite its limitations, however, deterrence will continue to be attractive for nonproliferation, if only because of the costs and risks of the alternatives: doing nothing (which allows a proliferator to develop weapons at will, a la North Korea), destroying a proliferator's capabilities (a la Israel's bombing of the Osirak and Al Kibar reactors or threatened U.S. and Israeli action against Iran, should it proliferate), or invasion (Iraq). Given the significant risk that terrorist acquisition of WMD continues to pose around the globe, the United States should focus particular attention on strengthening the network of legal controls, intelligence sharing, and international cooperation that prevent their spread and keep the risk well below the threshold of deterring use.

4. A NUCLEAR DETERRENT FOR THE 21st CENTURY

Clark A. Murdock

The Obama administration's policy from the outset has been to reduce U.S. reliance on nuclear weapons as a near-term step in the long-term pursuit of a world without nuclear weapons. This is easy for the United States to say, because it has the world's strongest military by far. If no one has nuclear weapons, the United States is the nondeterrable "600-pound gorilla." As Paul Bracken, who coined the term "the second nuclear age," observed in 2012: "China, Russia, India, Pakistan, North Korea, and Iran hardly desire a world that is 'safe' for U.S. strong-arm tactics with conventional forces." For nations wanting the same freedom of action that our conventional superiority gives us, giving up the nuclear option makes no sense.

Much like the United States in the 1950s when it faced massive Warsaw Pact conventional forces, other states are increasing their reliance on nuclear weapons. Russia and China are embarked on aggressive nuclear modernization programs; North Korea has joined the nuclear club; and Iran may be pursuing nuclear weapons. During the Cold War, the United States deployed about 7,000 tactical nuclear weapons in Europe, so that the Soviets would know that any major war in Europe would "go nuclear." Today, the Russian general staff is writing doctrine for how Russia could use nuclear weapons in a conflict with a conventionally superior force (that would be the U.S.-led NATO) to "deescalate" a crisis. Nuclear weapons offset conventional military superiority. When the U.S. military declares that it is seeking "full spectrum dominance" (see Joint Vision 2010), it simply reinforces the dependence of our would-be competitors on nuclear weapons.

How does the United States counter the nuclear weapons of other states that don't want to live under Pax Americana? We need to get serious again about nuclear weapons. The days of massive retaliation and mutual assured destruction are over, but nuclear weapons still matter for the United States because they are the most credible way of deterring how other countries might employ their nuclear weapons against us. The scenarios are different, and the stakes less existential. But we are in the second nuclear age, and denial is no longer an option.

Embrace Realism. The fallacy of hoping that our competitors would give up their means for offsetting U.S. conventional power is laid bare by the actions of Russia, China, and North Korea today. In the same way that the United States and the Soviet Union did during the Cold War, these states "use" their nuclear weapons every day. They understand that nuclear weapons are a primary element of the global distribution of power that provides the underlying structure for deterrence relationships between all states, not just those states seeking to oppose the United States. They also know that their nuclear weapons will cast a "nuclear shadow" over any major conflict with the United States. During the first nuclear age, it was the mutual fear of nuclear escalation that kept the Cold War cold as the two global superpowers engaged in Thomas Schelling's "competition in risk-taking." And as they plan for how to cope with a United States that increasingly acts as if nuclear war is unthinkable, they are thinking through how they might physically employ a nuclear weapon to demonstrate their willingness to escalate to the nuclear level. For these conventionally weaker powers, it won't be as a last resort, because a lengthy conventional war with the United States is a no-win proposition. "Going nuclear" early in a conflict in a manner that convinces the United States to back off (but does not provoke us into "going ballistic") makes sense from their perspective. We need to internalize that and plan accordingly.

Buy 21st-Century Nukes, not Cold War Ones. Sustaining a U.S. nuclear force designed for the Cold War cannot be the right response to the challenges of "the second nuclear age." Like our potential adversaries, we should develop and procure new nuclear weapons. We also need nuclear weapons whose employment demonstrates our willingness (if necessary) to break the nuclear threshold in a manner that does not set off uncontrollable nuclear escalation. From a global perspective, we need to maintain nuclear parity with the Russians and sustain nuclear superiority over the Chinese—dealing with a Russia that thought it had nuclear superiority would be even more difficult than it already is; a China that had achieved nuclear parity would tear big holes in the U.S. nuclear umbrella. Our conventional superiority obviates some of our requirements for nuclear weapons, but it creates others. This is paradoxical, to be sure, but paradoxes seem endemic to any nuclear era.

5. DETERRENCE IN THE CYBER AGE

James A. Lewis

Deterrence is the threat to use military force to impose intolerable costs if an opponent takes an unacceptable action. The threat must be credible, which requires opponents to calculate whether it is serious and if potential gains outweigh the possible harm. The context for deterrence has changed markedly, from a single peer opponent to several different rivals, each with different capabilities and tolerance for risk.

Nuclear weapons form the core of strategic deterrence, but their utility is increasingly constrained. "First strikes" are stigmatized, as is nuclear weapons use for anything other than to deter nuclear attack. The destructive effect of nuclear weapons is disproportional to the attacks we face, reducing the credibility of threats to use them. Nuclear weapons deter nuclear attack and (with general military forces) major conventional war, but there is little between these two extremes.

The likelihood that a country will carry out its deterrent threat depends on both material and political factors. Powerful militaries can inflict immense harm even without nuclear weapons, and no one doubts the capabilities of U.S. forces. Opponents use several techniques to manage and reduce the risk of retaliation, such as relying on proxy forces and irregulars. Opponents can limit their actions to those that do not qualify as the use of force (defined by the UN Charter as threatening a nation's territorial integrity or political independence) or that threaten

American lives or major economic damage (the U.S. threshold for preemptive response to cyber attack) and diminish the likelihood of American retaliation.

This could be proof that deterrence works now much as it did during the Cold War and is effective at a "strategic" level. America's military rivals avoid actions that could trigger a damaging U.S. military response. It also suggests the limits of deterrence. Opponents likely calculate that actions that do not affect America's vital national interests, as they perceive them, will not trigger a damaging response.

The United States could change these calculations if it convinced opponents that it had an expansive definition of vital national interests, such as defending the "global commons," but these broad definitions are unpersuasive. Other countries define vital national interests in a more limited fashion and it is through this narrower prism that they measure U.S. pronouncements. For extended deterrence, we can likely deter opponents from invasion or nuclear attacks on allies or friends, but not from supporting terror attacks by proxies or most kinds of cyber attack.

When it comes to a deterrent threat, nuclear weapons are too much; launching a few random cruise missiles is too little; perhaps threatening cyber attack can reshape opponent calculations? This idea is better in theory than in practice. If deterrence has to threaten unacceptable cost, cyber attacks cannot deliver. Their effect is tactical, and while they offer real military utility, they do not pose an existential threat or create intolerable costs. A stand-alone cyber attack like Stuxnet would create only temporary annoyance, and annoyance is not an astute strategy.

"Cross-domain" deterrence is another twist on traditional nuclear deterrence. The idea is to threaten that an attack by an opponent in one domain—for instance, on U.S. space or cyber assets—will result in damaging counterattacks in another domain—such as against sea or land targets. However, cross-domain deterrence turns out to be unworkable. How many ATMs must Iran hack to justify a cruise missile response? How much stolen intellectual property justifies a strike against a Chinese space launch facility? Cross-domain deterrence's complicated strategic calculus does not produce credible threats.

Some scholars argue that a lower threshold for the use of force in cyberspace could deter cyber attack. China's cyber espionage, they say, is "death by 1,000 cuts," and justifies retaliation as economic espionage imperceptibly saps vital industrial capabilities. There is no evidence that the Chinese follow this strategy, which sounds more like the plot of a cheap thriller. Nor have the 1,000 cuts done much harm—America continues to grow, and if growth has been slow in the last 15 years, it reflects bad policy choices more than nefarious foreign stratagems. In any case, after Snowden, it would be unwise for the United States to insist that cyber espionage is an act of war.

Deterrence worked best when linked to clear foreign policy goals and red lines, such as shielding Europe from invasion. Weak linkages between deterrent threats and vital American interests make red lines unpersuasive and encourage opponents to calculate how much they can get away with. The circumstances where the United States will inflict unacceptable harm on an opponent (and risk harm to itself) remain very few.

A vast range of coercive activities directed against the United States and its allies are not deterrable. Some of these actions have only symbolic effect, such as blocking a bank's website. Other actions advance regional agendas that may appear to opponents an peripheral to U.S. vital interests. Some actions, like cyber espionage, fall outside of the scope of what international law regards as justifying the use of retaliatory force. The United States can no more deter espionage or proxy conflict now than it could in the Cold War. Rather than ask what we can deter, it is better to ask how to clearly define vital interests and plan how to counter opponents who adjust their strategies to rely on techniques and technologies that avoid triggering a U.S. military response.

6. THE ROLE OF CONVENTIONAL FORCES IN DETERRENCE

Maren Leed

For decades, U.S. conventional forces' primary role in deterrence has been to maintain sufficient capability and capacity to engage in a large-scale, potentially long-duration fight with other large conventional forces. While nuclear forces remained the "ultimate" deterrent, conventional U.S. capability was one in the range of challenges an adversary might face when contemplating actions contrary to U.S. national interests.

Since the collapse of the Soviet Union, and especially in the 21st century, the deterrence picture has become more complex in at least two ways. First, the Bush doctrine of preemption has given way to conventional wisdom that claims that Americans are no longer willing to support large-scale employment of U.S. forces. (This view is borne out by the inability or unwillingness of the U.S. Congress to reverse defense budget cuts, despite numerous and growing demands for U.S. military capabilities around the globe.) A second shift relates to the growing power of non-state actors, from terrorists to criminal networks to pirates, whose deterrence calculi have proven different than those with which many U.S. strategists had become familiar.

Both changes—domestic reluctance to employ large U.S. military forces, and their more limited salience to the full range of complex challenges facing U.S. leaders—affect the basic calculus of deterrence, which is a function of both will and capacity. Political constraints affect the "will" component, and the ability of non-state and irregular actors to pose asymmetric threats to conventional forces affects the relevance of their capacity. Given this reality, questions about how much of a role conventional forces can play in future deterrence strategies are well warranted.

It would be foolish, however, to underestimate their continued relevance. It is important to note that the large, near-peer state competitors for which conventional U.S. forces have been principally designed remain strong, and at least one is growing stronger. This reality implies that capacity will continue to be needed. That said, however, different and smaller capabilities may be more relevant to deterring other threats. The larger question with respect to potential U.S. adversaries is about will: not only whether U.S. leaders would commit forces if required, but, more importantly, whether others perceive that they would.

Here, the U.S. government has been clearly signaling its desire to keep its military commitments limited, and when commitment is absolutely necessary, small. While this is an accurate reflection of public desires, the question for U.S. leaders is whether more can be done within the "limited and small" framework to enhance the U.S. deterrent posture. For example, Russia's move into Crimea was essentially a fait accompli by the time U.S. forces were deployed on the ground. Could the small units of U.S. forces that deployed to Poland and the Baltic states have been positioned earlier as indications of Russian troop movements became clear? Elsewhere in the world, the tinderboxes in the South and East China Seas could flare at any moment. Should U.S. leaders be routinely approving freedom-of-navigation operations in the South and East China Seas as a demonstration of American commitment to international maritime norms and a political solution to maritime disputes in the region?

Such actions would of course involve risks. Employing forces proactively—however small—runs the risk that if others take actions against them, the United States could be drawn further into conflagrations it might prefer to handle differently. Setting "trip wires," like red lines, only serves to deter if, when tripped, the consequences are quick and severe. On the other hand, taking more visible though tailored steps might change the trajectory of certain conflicts, forestalling larger problems and potential calls for more significant U.S. military intervention later on. Such actions could align more clearly with current U.S. public will. The capacity question—whether U.S. conventional capabilities are well suited to deter non-state actors—is more complex. In both instances, however, a more robust cost-benefit analysis of the degree to which smaller conventional force formations might better contribute to current deterrence challenges is both necessary and overdue.

7. THE CHALLENGE OF DETERRING ISIS

Thomas M. Sanderson

Through its coalition against ISIS, the West and its local allies are struggling to save a region now teetering on the edge of a geopolitical precipice. The amalgam of coalition forces—much of it still notional—is an engineer's nightmare: composed of countless moving parts of marginal quality, with American pressure and a fear of ISIS as its only lubricants. The U.S.-led force also confronts an unpalatable reality: the adversary is undeterrable.

Foreign fighters pouring over Turkey's border to do battle in Syria can make one final stop before gliding through the Bab Al-Salam gate. Before a perfunctory wave through by border officials, aspiring jihadists can sell their passports to a well-positioned café owner who knows these fighters will never again need them. Drawn from a life of marginalization to one of empowerment and eventual salvation, dozens of young men will transform themselves into human bombs at the direction of ISIS or Jabhat al-Nusra.

Seemingly inexhaustible in number, Sunni boys and men from America to Indonesia and more than 75 countries in between are drawn by the dramatic imagery, fueled by social media, of heroic fighters doing battle against all manner of evil. These young men—many of them illiterate and poor—move from a life devoid of choice, dignity, and respect to an environment impervious to reason and fear. A long-sought caliphate is in place, they are told, and it needs defending at all costs.

Willing to die in defense of their religion and the self-declared caliph who interprets it for them, many of these fighters are energized by the promise of a favorable postmortem evaluation of their Earthly deeds. Helping to cleanse holy lands of corrupt, despotic, Western-controlled Sunni governments (and even more detestable Shi'a regimes) is intoxicating indeed. The excesses and failures of corrupt governments have thrust them—fearless and energized—to the front lines of a holy war.

For some of those who do not perish on the battlefield, their onward movement presents an entirely new threat. At times withdrawing through the same border crossing in Turkey, there is the option of buying a now-repurposed passport for travel to Europe. Chances are, the documents on offer were once held by some of the estimated 3,000 European fighters who journeyed to the region, many hailing from one of 30 U.S. "visa-waiver" countries. Soon they could be on an airplane to America—intentions unknown, but quite likely lethal.

What can be done about ISIS and its team of motivated, trained foreign fighters and other non-state actors like them? Is the only solution arrest or death, or can those two sanctions prevent them from taking up arms in the first place?

Unfortunately, a deterrence strategy, which by definition is based on the threat of consequences, is unlikely to succeed in the fight against ISIS or similarly minded groups. Death is a goal for many jihadists, and one to be celebrated. With few deterrent options, the United States and its partners should support efforts aimed at dissuading would-be fighters before they make the decision to join ISIS. This may include local efforts to engage family members, clergy, community leaders, and law enforcement, who in turn can discourage plans by those most at risk to fight and die in Syria or Iraq. These influences must be brought to bear before an ISIS commander or facilitator makes his mark on the individual over social media or in person. After that point, stemming the flow of fighters will be much harder and more expensive to achieve.

PART II

What Are the Implications of Putin's New Russia?

8. RUSSIA'S INFLUENCE ON EUROPE

Heather A. Conley

The transatlantic community awoke on March 18, 2014, to a strategic surprise: the Russian Federation, a "strategic partner" of the European Union, had formally annexed Crimea. This was an event not seen since Adolf Hitler annexed Austria in 1938. On that same day, Vladimir Putin articulated a new guiding doctrine for Russian foreign policy, stating that Moscow will preemptively act to "protect" ethnic Russians wherever they live. This policy became reality as Russia quickly moved to destabilize eastern Ukraine in support of pro-Russian separatists.

The post–Cold War era and order has come to an abrupt end. We have yet to identify what this new period will bring. What does the future hold and how should the transatlantic community respond to Russian malfeasance in its neighborhood? What are Putin's long-term intentions? How do regional leaders perceive Russian actions? What transatlantic policy responses will be most effective with regard to sanctions, energy, civil society, and defense? Perhaps most importantly, can Europe and the transatlantic alliance hold together despite Russia's pervasive economic and political influence within the European Union?

As this collection goes to print, the Russian flag still flies over Simferopol, the capital of Crimea; the conflict in Ukraine's Donbas region is now Europe's latest and greatest frozen conflict; and the United States and Europe have yet to fully address the growing threat that Putin's revanchist ambitions pose.

When Central and Eastern Europe threw off the Communist yoke and the Soviet Union collapsed, Europe and the United States transformed their Soviet policy of isolation and containment to one of political and economic integration with the Russian Federation. This approach had been largely successful over the past 25 years. Russia joined the Group of Eight (G8) in 1998, the World Trade Organization in 2012, and was considered for membership in the Organization for Economic Cooperation and Development (OECD).

In the past 10 years alone, the value of Russia's global trade has nearly quadrupled from $210 billion in 2003 to $802 billion in 2013. Last year, Russia's trade with the EU represented 48.5 percent of its total. Although U.S.-Russian trade ties remained subdued by comparison, the two former superpowers developed a measurable degree of economic interdependence, as evidenced by the International Space Station and Russian-made titanium for Boeing's 787 fleet. This transatlantic policy of integration came to an abrupt halt on March 18, 2014.

Over time, Russia's economic integration with Europe—and specifically with the countries of Central and Eastern Europe—has gradually devolved from a positive source of growth into a negative and corrosive force, serving only to widen economic and political rifts within Europe. Europe's reliance on Russian energy and financial resources and its accompanied political influence has hindered its ability to formulate a swift, unified, and robust response to Moscow's violation of Ukraine's territorial integrity. Europe's policy hesitancy is in actuality a delicate political balancing act in which Europe must weigh the normative benefits of defending international legal principles against the tangible, self-inflicted economic costs of imposing sanctions against Russia. While Europe's sustained sanctions campaign has seemingly tipped the scales in favor of democratic principles for the time being, its asymmetrical economic impacts are raising questions about the durability of this commitment. Nowhere else is this equilibrium teetering more than in Central and Eastern Europe where Russia has begun to reclaim its influence.

Presciently, in a July 2009 Open Letter to President Obama, a group of pro-American leaders from Central and Eastern Europe, such as former Polish President Lech Walesa, foreshadowed the dark side of Russia's integration with the West: "Russia is back as a revisionist power pursuing a 19th-century agenda with 21st-century tactics and methods.... It [Russia] uses overt and covert means of economic warfare, ranging from energy blockades and politically motivated investments to bribery and media manipulation in order to advance its interests and to challenge the transatlantic orientation of Central and Eastern Europe." Despite being full-fledged members of the European Union for over a decade, the countries of Central Europe are experiencing an erosion of the rule of law and good governance.

Freedom House's 2013 Nations in Transit report noted that only two (Latvia and the Czech Republic) out of 10 Central European countries have improved their democracy "score card" after being members of NATO and the European Union for over a decade. The other eight countries' ratings dropped in the areas of media freedom, electoral processes, judicial independence, and corruption. Increasingly, there appears to be a strong correlation between a marked decline in transparency, rule of law, and democratic practices, and the extent of Russian economic and political engagement in these countries.

In the case of Bulgaria, recent media reports estimated that as much as one-third of Bulgaria's economy is owned by Russian entities, with particular concentration in the energy, financial, and media sectors. Bulgaria's political landscape is highly volatile and opaque; the country has already seen four governments in the past two years. Consequently, Transparency International ranked Bulgaria 77 out of 177 countries on perceived levels of public-sector corruption—the second lowest in the European Union.

There also appears to be a linkage between Russian influence and the rise of populist, nationalistic, and xenophobic political parties as many of these entities receive financial support from Russian-affiliated nongovernmental organizations (NGOs).

Taking advantage of Europe's economic malaise, these increasingly successful fringe parties have contributed to the weakening of political support for the European Union and governments across Europe. Their impacts, however, are most evident in the former Eastern Bloc, where institutions and civil society remain underdeveloped and susceptible to the revitalization of former Soviet networks.

In the case of Hungary, many of these trends have toxically blended to produce an increasingly authoritarian regime. Over the last decade, Hungary has maintained strong economic and political ties with Russia. Russia is Hungary's largest trading partner outside the European Union, and the country remains 80 percent reliant on Russian energy. As Russia's grasp on Hungary's economy has tightened, nationalist and xenophobic groups—such as the neo-fascist Jobbik party—have also risen to prominence, further undermining the country's Western, liberal orientation. Moreover, Hungarian Prime Minister Viktor Orban has articulated a significant shift in national direction and policy orientation, declaring in July that Hungary must strive to build "an illiberal new state based on national foundations" as evidenced by legislative motions to restrict free speech (including an oppressive advertising tax), centralize authority (Hungary's new constitution has been amended five times), and erode the independence of the judiciary. Noting that the geopolitical "wind is blowing from the East," Orban has credited Moscow for these latest Russian-styled Hungarian "reforms."

These illiberal trends have been accompanied by distinctly pro-Russian foreign policies in Budapest. Orban has consistently derided the EU's sanctions against Russia, and Hungary abruptly discontinued its sale of excess gas supplies to Ukraine after a visit from the CEO of Gazprom this fall. Hungary received a 10 billion euro loan from Russia for a new nuclear power plant facility, increasing Hungary's energy dependence on Russian technology and financial support. Negative developments in Hungary and its neighbors threaten to derail wider European efforts to restrain Russian recidivism.

Although the 21st-century East-West confrontation does not bear the ideological vestiges of the Cold War, there is a clear ideological component. This contestation is between liberal versus illiberal, transparency and good governance versus corruption and "managed democracy." The unqualified success of Central Europe's transformation from Communism to liberal democracies and market economies is not immutable, and we should not trick ourselves into believing it is so.

9. PUTIN'S DILEMMA

Andrew C. Kuchins

Just days before Boris Yeltsin shocked the world by retiring early from the Russian presidency on December 31, 1999—making then-Prime Minister Vladimir Putin acting president—Putin released his Millennial Statement that outlined Russia's immense challenges and a vision for its future. This vision emphasized greater predictability, prosperity, and stability for Russia after the economically and socially traumatic 1990s. The document's other core theme was the urgent need to reconsolidate the Russian state in order to lead the recovery of the Russian nation.

For the past 15 years that Putin has served as Russia's de jure and/or de facto national leader, the majority of Russian people have been satisfied that he has delivered what he promised and what they want. During his first two terms as president, the Russian economy grew at approximately 7 percent per year (measured in nominal dollar terms and accounting for ruble appreciation, the figure is an impressive 26 percent). Even after the global economic crisis in 2008–2009, the Russian economy regained its footing, growing at a rate of more than 4 percent in 2010 and 2011.

The foundation for Vladimir Putin's consistently high political ratings has been the Russian people's perception that their economic prospects were constantly improving. Putin's so-called vertical of power—an increasingly state-centric political economy—has been facilitated by a growing economic pie that could be carved up and distributed to Putin loyalists. This system, patrimonial authoritarianism, finds its historical roots traced to the princes of Muscovy, Russian tsars, and later Soviet general secretaries. In this sense, Vladimir Putin is a very traditional Russian leader.

But signs that not all was well in modern Muscovy manifested themselves in the winter of 2011–2012 when the largest political demonstrations took place in Russia in 20 years as tens of thousands of protesters took to the streets to condemn the falsified Duma elections of December 2011. Putin's United Russia party fared poorly in those elections, marking Putin's first electoral defeat since his emergence on the national stage a decade earlier. The demonstrations also marked the first large social media-mobilized opposition Putin had ever faced. It seemed clear from private discussions with Putin and his inner circle prior to the 2011 election that Putin was taken by surprise. The demonstrations were a shock to Putin personally as well as to the political system he oversaw for over a decade.

While the protesters were ideologically diverse, the majority were the relatively well-off middle and upper-middle classes who had benefited the most during those prosperous years of Putin's tenure. But they viewed Moscow's centralized, corrupt, and authoritarian political system nurtured by Putin as incapable of promoting further economic growth or answering their demands for improved governance.

When he returned to the presidency in May 2012, Putin faced a difficult choice as signs of economic stagnation were already visible: he could either co-opt the growing middle class by addressing their concerns and embark on structural economic reforms or risk undermining the political foundation of his vertical of power.

Putin's dilemma is reminiscent of the Soviet Politburo in the early 1980s. Despite massive windfall revenue of petrodollars, the economy was so structurally inefficient that the Soviet growth rate was close to zero. At the high point of Soviet zastoi or stagnation, Brezhnev and his successors decided structural economic reform was too politically risky and attempted to muddle through. Had oil prices remained high, muddling may have been successful and the Soviet Union would have endured. Of course, oil prices plummeted, the Soviet Union attempted reform, and collapse ensued.

Putin, like his Soviet predecessors, has avoided reform and the Russian economy has continued to stagnate (1.3 percent growth in 2013) even before Crimea annexation and the war in Ukraine despite historically high oil prices. It appeared that Putin had already decided to abandon economic growth and prosperity as the foundation for his political popularity and authority. This risky political strategy would require a new political narrative to justify his indefinite leadership if economic growth and prosperity were no longer the essential thread.

This new political narrative began to form in 2012–2013 with a growing emphasis on traditional Russian values captured in the 19th-century Russian policy of "official nationality" revolving around the triptych of autocracy, orthodoxy, and Russian nationality. The crisis over Ukraine offered an ideal opportunity to further consolidate this new political narrative. Previously, Putin had always been careful to avoid enflaming Russian nationalism, but his seminal speech to the Russian Assembly formally annexing Crimea on March 18, however, articulated a highly chauvinistic form of Russian nationalism that does not accept the legitimacy of post–1991 borders let alone post–World War II and even post–World War I borders.

Putin has reintroduced the Tsarist-era term of Novorossiya, which geographically included much of Eastern and Southern Ukraine under the administrative jurisdiction of Russia. This has become his new political narrative and a rallying cry for the insurgents in Eastern Ukraine.

Putin will manage the devastating economic consequences of his strategic choice in many different ways. The nearly 25 percent decline in oil prices has put further pressure on his government. The house arrest in September of leading economic magnate Vladimir Yevtushenkov sent a deep chill through the

Russian business community in a similar manner as the 2003 arrest of Mikhail Khodorkovsky. The Khodorkovsky affair and the destruction of the Yukos oil company was the watershed event in the establishment of Putin's vertical of power, including the redistribution of some of the core assets of the Russian economy.

As the economic pie is reduced, Putin must find ways to assure the loyalty of his core allies and the intelligence services to guarantee his leadership. All signs suggest that another redistribution of assets to his loyalists is underway. Western sanctions may actually help facilitate this process as Western financial institutions and individual investors are removed as arbiters in the Russian market that make it easier for erstwhile Putin allies to consume their own.

Putin clearly has made a Faustian bargain with Russian nationalism and oligarchic predators with unpredictable consequences for Russia's neighbors, regional security, and the Russian people. Although government officials and experts perceive that Russia is weak, Putin has proven himself time and time again as highly adept at playing what appears to be a weak hand. Ukrainian President Petro Poroshenko has described Putin as "unpredictable, emotional, and dangerous." How long Putin can manage this volatile situation that he has created is an open question, but we should not assume it will be brief or that whoever comes after Putin will be easier.

10. THE CALCULATIONS OF RUSSIA'S NEIGHBORS

Jeffrey Mankoff

For Russia's neighbors in the South Caucasus and Central Asia, the Ukraine crisis is a watershed moment. Since independence, these countries had pursued a "multi-vector" foreign policy, which meant seeking new partnerships while acknowledging their dependence on Russia and being careful to respect Russian red lines.

After the annexation of Crimea and destabilization of eastern Ukraine, the location of those red lines no longer seems clear. The resulting uncertainty is forcing the leaders of the South Caucasus and Central Asian states to be more deferential to Moscow in the near term while accelerating these states' efforts to loosen and diversify their ties with Moscow. Time, especially the emergence of a new generation of leaders with no memories of the Soviet Union, will only accelerate this process.

Before the outbreak of protests on Kyiv's Maidan Nezalezhnosti [Independence Square] in September 2013, Ukraine's strategy for dealing with Russia was multi-vector as well. Economic and cultural ties with Russia remained strong, but the government, even under the allegedly pro-Russian President Viktor Yanukovych (whose political career the Kremlin aided), sought to develop diplomatic, trade, and investment ties with other partners. For Ukraine, that meant primarily the European

Union, while the South Caucasus and Central Asian states have looked variously to the United States, EU, Turkey, China, and elsewhere.

While these states pursued economic ties with a range of neighbors, they understood that Moscow regarded security co-operation, especially the presence of NATO or U.S. forces, as a red line, and steered clear—or paid the price. Georgia's courting of NATO, which contributed to the 2008 war with Russia, and Kyrgyzstan's hosting of U.S. forces at the Manas Transit Center, which helped fuel Moscow's role in ousting former President Kurmanbek Bakiyev, served as object lessons of the costs of seeking outside security assurances. Still, the rule seemed to be: trade with whomever you want at least as long as you do not challenge Russia's preferred position such as in EU energy markets, but keep U.S. and NATO forces out.

In line with this understanding, before the Maidan protests, post-Soviet elites from other states were generally weary of joining the Russian-backed Eurasian Customs Union with Belarus and Kazakhstan, or the planned Eurasian Economic Union. Despite the fact that Kazakh President Nursultan Nazarbayev first proposed the Eurasian Union in the 1990s, many Kazakh officials and businessmen opposed Putin's scheme, and even Nazarbayev took pains to emphasize that the planned body was solely an economic union.

Others, including Armenia, where more than 5,000 Russian troops are based, as well as Kyrgyzstan and Tajikistan, whose economies are heavily dependent on remittances from Russia, demurred. Meanwhile, Ukraine, along with Armenia, Georgia, and Moldova, negotiated association agreements with the EU that, when implemented, would radically transform their economic and administrative structures, weakening inherited links with Russia. Although Moscow opposed these agreements and encouraged its neighbors to join its customs union, these countries largely continued charting their own course, mostly evincing little interest in the customs union.

Nevertheless, in the run-up to the EU summit where Armenia,

Georgia, Moldova, and Ukraine were set to formalize their association agreements, Russia began exerting enormous political and economic pressure. In September, Armenia abruptly announced it was shelving its association agreement and would join the customs union. Soon thereafter, Ukrainian President Yanukovych also buckled, following a secretive two-day visit to Moscow. Yanukovych's about-face sparked the protests that led to his downfall, Russia's occupation of Crimea, and the insurgency in eastern Ukraine. These events seemed at odds with the previously accepted rules of the game. Russia's military intervention in Ukraine was driven more by post-colonial disregard than any prospect of NATO forces on its border (indeed, it was the Russian intervention that led new President Petro Poroshenko to again seek Ukrainian NATO membership).

Moreover, to justify the intervention, Putin proclaimed a wide-ranging mandate to protect "compatriots," "Russians and Russian-speakers" throughout the former USSR. This formula gave Moscow a pretext to intervene in any of its former dependencies—including the Baltic states. Incautious remarks from Putin about Kazakhstan lacking historical legitimacy only exacerbated the sense of concern in the neighborhood that Russia had gone rogue.

The Ukraine crisis held another lesson for the former Soviet states as well, a lesson about the dangers of "people power." The "Maidan scenario"—a corrupt, ineffective government thrown out by its own people—represents the greatest fear of many post-Soviet leaders. The result, in at least some states, has been greater repression and less openness, even if these crackdowns make a Maidan more likely in the longer term.

In the near term, the twin fear of Moscow and the Maidan is working to Russia's advantage. Unlike the West, Russia will not object to crackdowns on domestic opposition, while joining the Eurasian Economic Union provides some insurance against Russian meddling (a krysha, or roof, in Russian criminal slang). In the past year, Armenia and Kyrgyzstan have applied to join the Eurasian Economic Union, while Azerbaijan and Georgia have increasingly hedged their pro-Western orientations. Further driving this tilt toward Moscow is the perception, widespread especially in Central Asia, that U.S. engagement in the region is declining with the withdrawal from Afghanistan.

Yet the post–Soviet states view Russia's decision to change the rules of the game as a threat to their sovereignty. The crisis in Ukraine has strained the bonds of affection tying these states to Russia. While they may have little choice but to join Russian-led multilateral bodies, these countries will work to ensure that these entities remain toothless, and will redouble their efforts to reduce their dependence on and vulnerability to Russia. Almost without exception, elites in the South Caucasus and Central Asia see greater U.S. engagement as vital to the sovereignty and independence of the region's states.

The irony is that, as Putin made clear in 2008, Russia does not view Ukraine, any more than the states of the South Caucasus and Central Asia, as a "real state." By forcing these countries to defend their independence, Moscow is compelling them to define themselves and their national interests, often in opposition to Russia. Russia's actions are breeding a new national identity and pride, which will be the surest guarantee of these countries' sovereignty over the longer term.

11. UKRAINE'S TRANSITION

Sarah Mendelson

The guiding aspiration since World War II and the mantra since the end of the Cold War for Euro-Atlantic security has been "Europe whole and free." For many, that conception of security has included an independent, democratic, and prosperous Ukraine. At times, improbable as it now seems, it has also included a democratic Russia.

What is to be done, as we pass the 25th anniversary of the fall of the Berlin Wall, with the 40th anniversary of the Helsinki Accords looming, about Vladimir Putin overseeing an invasion of Ukraine and a war that has cost thousands of lives? Setting aside armed intervention, what is the right response given his apparent judgment that the post–Cold War order is not to his liking, and universal rights, transparency, and accountability are either deemed not applicable to Russia or threaten its sovereignty? Are we all doomed to live in a new, post–Helsinki world?

The answer better be no or we will see more chaos and violence in Europe. The need for coherent, coordinated support to Ukraine has vaulted to the top of the Euro-Atlantic security agenda for 2015. Political transitions are complicated enough without a neighbor trying to split the country and occupy territory. But a year after the Euromaidan first formed, it is important to remember that Ukrainian citizens chose and drove this transition and still do. The stakes are especially high; this is Ukraine's third go at post–independence transformation, and many believe it is their last chance at creating a stable, law-governed country.

In responding to this urgent agenda, we need to identify and apply lessons learned from decades of support to political transitions around the world.

LESSONS LEARNED

In contrast to the cartoonish images that some paint of how international democracy promotion works, we cannot want democracy and rule of law in Ukraine more than Ukrainians do. We ought to have both a sense of humility at outsiders' ability to effect change and a highly nuanced understanding of Ukrainian public opinion. According to a September 2014 International Republican Institute (IRI) poll, Ukraine is neither as deeply divided as some argue, nor as uniform as others suggest. More and different data are needed for a fuller understanding of Ukrainian political demands. Using data to address citizen needs is critical to reducing conflict, countering propaganda from Moscow, and addressing historical grievances—so often overlooked or underappreciated as drivers of development.

Euro-Atlantic cohesion is also vital to effective support of Ukraine, and when divisions emerge, U.S. and European diplomats must make it a priority to mend them. Russia actively tries to divide and conquer; there are illiberal trend lines in Hungary and other European Union countries. With the departure of both Swedish Foreign Minister Carl Bilt and Polish Foreign Minister Radoslaw Sikorski, strong voices in support of Ukraine and Euro-Atlantic cohesion, there is heightened need for both continued U.S. diplomatic attention to these issues and new European voices to emerge.

As we speak with one voice, we must not become overly focused on any one political figure. Unconditional political devotion to Boris Yeltsin as he failed to deliver to his citizens cost the United States enormously in terms of credibility in Russia. Instead, our support must go to those in Ukraine who listen and respond to citizens' needs.

Euromaidan activists argue the task at hand is moving from "the revolution of dignity" to "the revolution of effectiveness." This requires transparency in budgets and accountability of officials; it is good news that the new laws on anticorruption were (finally) adopted. They must now be implemented. The activists also acknowledge that broader behavioral change across Ukraine needs to occur in terms of demand for transparency and accountability. Currently tied with the Central African Republic, Iran, and Nigeria in terms of corruption, Ukraine needs to apply the comprehensive approach to tackling corruption that Georgia deployed in recent years. Nothing less will work and requires political will from both society and government.

The Kremlin has successfully weaponized information, even going so far as to take over television stations in Ukraine at gun point. The importance of getting accurate information both to Russians and to countering more globally the disinformation supported by Kremlin-financed platforms should be a high priority. Are companies that include the RT news channel in cable packages in the United States and Europe enabling Kremlin propaganda, and if so, what can be done about it? While the U.S. Broadcasting Board of Governors' recently launched 30-minute Russian-language television news program "Current Time" is laudable, much more is needed to counter the steady stream of falsehoods propagated by the Kremlin. Specifically, the traditional approaches to supporting independent media need to be brought quickly into the 21st century, including tapping millennials to creatively advance information on new platforms as well as on television. A gathering of stakeholders on this issue ought to be convened in Europe in early 2015.

Finally, foreign assistance absent home-grown strategy is not going to solve Ukraine's problems. Prime Minister Arseniy Yatsenyuk's "Recovery for Ukraine: Action Plan" is a good start. While the United States allocated around $291 million this year for democracy, economic, and security efforts, President Petro Poroshenko and the new Parliament need to draft a compelling and transparent account of what funding is needed for what programs, including a long-term plan for energy independence. The sources of revenue should be varied and include the assets stolen by senior members of the Yanukovich government, apparently in the tens of billions of dollars. The location and return of these funds are rightly a priority, however laborious to track.

BEHAVIOR HAS CONSEQUENCES

Rather wobbly in the beginning, the United States and Europe have demonstrated good solidarity on Ukraine since the downing of Malaysia Airlines Flight 17 and the incursion of thousands of Russian troops into Eastern Ukraine in late August. Putin counts on this fading over time. Instead, 2015 needs to be a year of unprecedented Euro-Atlantic cohesion; it is our best shot at shaping not only Putin's choices, but those of the Russian elite, some of whom might—just might—emerge as a counterbalance. A few reports suggest that fissures are emerging in Moscow, a by-product of the bite from sanctions, which need to stay in place.

In the longer run, and most important, is the demonstration effect that a prosperous and open new Ukraine might eventually have on Russia. Even after two decades of disappointment on the democracy front in Russia, there is still a minority that wants to be part of the West, wants to have a "normal" life with a government responsive to its citizens, and institutions that deliver. Ukraine's path, if able to choose for itself, could help shape Russia's future; indeed that is what Putin fears and why it matters for Euro-Atlantic security.

12. A TEST OF WILLS ON SANCTIONS

Juan C. Zarate

For all the costs that Western sanctions and lower oil prices are inflicting on the Russian economy, the Russian flag still flies over Crimea, Moscow remains undeterred, and the September 5, 2014, ceasefire in Ukraine has failed to end the fighting in Eastern Ukraine. In response, Russia is using its own form of economic and energy warfare as both a shield and a sword. This all suggests that there are limits to the West's ability to deter Russian aggression.

Since Russia's annexation of Crimea in March, Western strategy has focused on blocking future deals with the Russian military sector, restricting Russian banks' access to long-term capital, depriving elements of the Russian oil sector of technology they need for offshore and shale drilling, and freezing the overseas assets of individuals tied to the Kremlin.

But most existing contracts between Western interests and their Russian clients have been allowed to continue. Rather than dealing an instant blow, the aim has been to starve the country of capital by sowing doubts among Western investors about the wisdom of investing in Russia. These efforts have produced tangible results, impacting Russia's ability to access the global banking and trade systems, and have already imposed direct transactional, investment, and reputational costs.

The capital constriction strategy appears to have been effective. Contracts and capital have evaporated, and Moscow has at-

43

tempted to dampen rumors that it could assert capital controls to halt the outflow of funds (net capital outflows are estimated to exceed $100 billion this year). The Russian Central Bank has been forced to intervene decisively in defense of the ruble as currency demand continues to plummet, spending $1.5 billion on October 8 alone. Growth has slowed to a near halt (projected to be just 0.4 percent for the year), and major Russian companies such as Aeroflot have been unable to acquire necessary investment.

Since Putin's return to the presidency, he has understood that Russia is economically vulnerable, and in recent years he has moved to reduce Russia's reliance on the dollar in international trade and finance. He also knew that there is a limit to the amount of financial pain that the West can inflict on a major economy with substantial economic and energy ties to Europe and the rest of the world. Russia's entanglements may be vulnerabilities, but they also allow Russia to exact a price of its own.

Companies subject to Western sanctions are making moves to circumvent the restrictions. Rosneft, the Russian oil company, is set to buy 30 percent of Norway's north Atlantic drilling, enabling it to access offshore drilling capabilities in the Arctic despite technology-export bans and financial restrictions. Meanwhile, Russian investors continue to deepen their economic interests in London, Frankfurt, and New York. And the Russian sovereign wealth fund and Russian pensions funds will be tapped for billions of dollars to shore up necessary capital requirements for its banks hit by sanctions.

Moscow is also responding to Western sanctions by substantially reducing flows of oil and gas to Ukraine, which restricts exports to other European customers as winter approaches. As some European countries have sent excess gas back to Ukraine in a reverse pipeline flow, Moscow has specifically punished these countries. For example, on October 2, Gazprom unexpectedly cut its supply of natural gas to Slovakia by 50 percent as punishment for this reverse flow. A recent visit by the CEO of Gazprom to Hungary completely ended Hungary's efforts to send gas to Ukraine.

The Kremlin has also banned agricultural imports from countries that have participated in the sanctions, which economically damages neighboring countries such as Poland and Finland. Symbolically, Russia has closed four McDonald's restaurants, citing health and sanitation reasons—a common Russian tactic when it seeks to punish a country or company. Moscow has frequently suggested that it will develop a national payment system that could replace Visa and MasterCard and they have threatened to prevent Western airlines from flying over Siberia to Asian destinations at great expense. American consulting and accounting firms could also be prevented from operating in Russia.

Russia has more cards to play. It could cut off supplies of engines to the U.S. space program. It is a big exporter of titanium and other resources needed by western companies and could restrict exports in retaliation. Moscow could emerge as a sanctions-busting financial partner to a country such as Iran, at the height of nuclear negotiations. Finally, in the past Russia has launched cyber-attacks against Estonia and Georgia as well as used tax and money-laundering investigations to silence critics. The Kremlin could enlist hackers and organized criminals to disrupt financial systems and companies in the West to complement the tit-for-tat sanctions war that has erupted. Some have questioned whether recent massive cyber-attacks against JP Morgan and others were Russian-originated due to events in Ukraine.

There are measures the West can take to minimize Russian countermeasures. Europe must finally take decisive measures to secure alternative sources of oil and gas. This will be a gradual shift, however, as Europe lacks the critical infrastructure necessary, particularly liquefied natural gas (LNG) facilities and alternative pipelines, to receive greater imports from abroad. Other countries should also seek diversity of Russian energy supply as Moscow becomes increasingly unpredictable.

New Russian investments in the United States and Europe also should be carefully scrutinized, and Western commercial contacts with suspect individuals and companies further constrained. There also needs to be a broader effort to marginalize illicit financial behavior—not just those individuals and entities tied to the invasion of Ukraine. Thus far, sanctions have been limited to targeted asset freezes, visa bans, and trade and financial restrictions in critical sectors.

A more robust sanctions campaign, however, would entail aggressive investigations of illicit financial activity of Russian interests globally—tied to concerns about money laundering, corruption, tax evasion, and links to Russian organized crime. This could include European measures to apply enhanced due diligence and reporting requirements on Russian entities or individuals with bank accounts or new investments in real estate. Europe applied similar scrutiny in Cyprus during its recent banking crisis but it must redouble its efforts.

But these steps would not be without complications. Distinguishing between legitimate and illicit financial activity would prove difficult. And at a time of weak growth, Europe has little appetite for additional economic pain. Already, existing sanctions have had tangible impacts on Europe's economy, impacting both large and small countries already struggling against a triple-dip recession.

At the end of the day, enduring the economic pain of sanctions for both Russia and the West is a test of wills. If one side is unwilling to endure the economic pain, the sanctions campaign will prove ineffective. At this moment, Moscow seems willing to accept the pain as it exerts its influence in its near abroad; the West also has accepted the cost to defend the international system, but it seems to do so with increasing reluctance. The West must realize that this crisis may be a new frozen economic conflict, where both sides use financial and economic tools to impose pain on the other. Both sides should prepare themselves for a long campaign.

13. ENERGY CODEPENDENCY

Edward C. Chow

During Vladimir Putin's first two terms as president of Russia from 1999 to 2008, oil prices rose from below $20 to over $140 per barrel. In many respects, this enabled the domestic and foreign policies that he pursued, including in the oil and gas industry where private ownership was restricted and the sector recentralized in the hands of the state and state companies. Today, Russia is more of a petro-state than the Soviet Union ever was, with oil and gas contributing more than a quarter of GDP, half of federal budget revenue, and two-thirds of the country's export earnings.

The same will not be true during Putin's third term as president from 2012 to 2018 as oil prices dropped below $90 per barrel from historic highs of above $100 for the last four years. For the energy industry, high prices eventually result in conservation, substitution, and new supply. The American shale gas and tight oil revolution is a classic example of the development of new supply. Even if this is a cyclical decline, oil prices are unlikely to return to the growth rate of the previous decade.

To maintain Russia's currently high oil and gas production and export levels on which its economy depends, large-scale and long-term investments are needed in exploration and development in frontier areas beyond Russia's traditional producing regions, such as in East Siberia and the Arctic offshore, and in costly infrastructure to bring new production from remote areas to markets in Russia or abroad. Majority state-owned Rosneft and Gazprom, or favored companies such as Novatek, needed Western energy partners to underwrite these investments and provide technical and management expertise. Western economic sanctions therefore come at a critical time for its oil and gas industry in response to Russia's aggression against Ukraine. Financial sanctions restrict access to capital for Russian energy companies. Sanctions against investments in frontier exploration in the Arctic offshore and shale oil have stalled or halted projects with major international oil companies.

The often-heard narrative that Europe is heavily dependent on Russian energy sources is true for some European countries yet Europe receives overall about 30 percent of its oil and gas imports from Russia. The less understood dynamic is that Russia is even more reliant on Europe as the market for 80 percent of its total oil and gas exports. While much has been made of Russia's recent energy mega-deals with China, diversification of Russia's export markets to Asia will take a decade or longer, if ever, to reach a level comparable to its exports to Europe. As global energy prices soften and global demand stagnates, Russia needs Europe more than ever as the primary destination of its oil and gas exports.

The other narrative is Russia's use of its oil and gas supplies as a tool of statecraft. In reality, Moscow has little room for maneuver. Europe will continue to import oil and gas from Russia; Russia cannot shift its oil and gas exports to Asia in the near term. Therefore, this boils down to the economic terms of energy trade, whether Europe and Russia are politically willing to lessen their degree of mutual dependence, and whether both sides are willing to bear the higher cost of supply diversification by shipping or receiving oil and gas over greater distances utilizing expensive new infrastructure.

Here natural gas matters a lot more than oil. As a globally traded commodity with ease of transportation, oil supply is much more flexible than gas supply, which is tied to fixed infrastructure and longer-term contracts in regionalized markets. In other words, Russia's oil pays the rent (at a ratio of 4 to 1, more valuable than gas), whereas gas is more about power politics—both domestic and foreign—as well as revenue generation and distribution.

For the third time in less than a decade, Europe is again faced with the possible interruption of Russian gas transiting Ukraine that, following the development of the Nord Stream pipeline, represents today around 15 percent of Europe's total gas supply. Each occasion was triggered by significant political developments in Ukraine that were perceived by Putin as affecting Russia's interests: the Orange Revolution (preceding the gas cutoff in 2006), the internal power struggle between President Yushchenko and Prime Minister Tymoshenko (the longer 2009 gas cutoff), and now the Euromaidan and the departure of former Ukrainian President Yanukovych (leading to the current standoff on gas supply). Each cutoff occurred during the winter months.

Neither Russia nor Ukraine can afford another gas crisis. Ukraine has yet to implement any fundamental reform of its dysfunctional and corrupt energy system. Reform requires political will on the part of Ukrainian leaders even under the most difficult conditions of war/insurrection and economic collapse and great patience by the Ukrainian people to accept increases in energy prices in order to improve energy efficiency and increase domestic production. Ukraine will require extensive financial assistance from international financial institutions and Western countries for the next five to ten years with strict reform conditionality.

As lower oil prices and Western sanctions exact a toll on Russia, Moscow will likely continue to see Ukraine as an undependable transit partner for its energy and to focus on completing its plan to bypass Ukraine entirely by constructing the South Stream gas pipeline system under the Black Sea and through the Balkans.

What role does Europe play as it enters potentially its third energy crisis with Russia? The European Union must decide to observe its own stated rules as outlined in the Third Energy Package and EU competition policies. After years of investigation of Gazprom's business practices in Europe, the "statement of objections" (or formal charge sheet) was poised to be released in May 2014. The matter is still pending. Europe must also decide whether and how to use its leverage to determine the terms of the gas trade with Russia. While creating a future EU "Energy Union" may be an important step, the EU must first implement its own rules rather than continually seek exemptions without reducing its energy vulnerabilities.

The best solution for all sides is for Russia and Ukraine to reach a six-month interim agreement, which is currently under discussion, on the gas debt that Ukraine owes Russia and on the gas price Russia will charge Ukraine. Continued brinksmanship between Russia and Ukraine on gas negotiations has only led to bad outcomes for all parties, including Europe.

14. NATO'S EASTERN FRONT

Andrew A. Michta

Faced with Russia's military aggression and its use of hybrid warfare in Ukraine, NATO remains caught in the double bind of shrinking defense resources and a continued lack of consensus on how to respond to this aggression beyond political condemnations, the imposition of economic sanctions, and enhanced exercise and readiness measures. NATO's new Eastern Front—consisting of the most active NATO members, the Baltic States, Poland, Romania, and Bulgaria—wants physical assurances that NATO will prevent potential Russian aggression, not reassurances that NATO will respond to aggression after it has occurred.

Herein lies the challenge: until NATO adequately shores up its Eastern Front with permanent military deployments, NATO's regional security and deterrent posture will continue to erode. Yet, several NATO countries insist that the permanent stationing of NATO forces near Russia's border not only would provoke additional Russian military action but also contravenes the 1997 NATO-Russia Founding Act (irrespective of Russia's own violation of this Act). NATO's easternmost states are also apprehensive about U.S. policy persistence and its sustained focus on Europe as events in the Middle East and the Asia-Pacific region draw attention and resources elsewhere. Against these political odds, establishing an effective deterrence regime against Russia along NATO's eastern frontier remains a daunting task.

It seems clear that Russian President Vladimir Putin's "Novorossiya" (or "New Russia") aims at reclaiming either direct or indirect Russian influence over the post–Soviet space—which could include NATO members Estonia, Lithuania, and Latvia. The immediate goal of Russia's irredentist policy in Ukraine is to maintain its hold on the east of Ukraine and to consolidate its gains there. The presence of Russian forces in Moldova, Georgia, and Armenia can be viewed as part of a larger Russian regional military strategy, likely to be accompanied by a gradual tightening of Russia's grip on other post–Soviet states.

The September 2014 NATO Summit in Newport, Wales, demonstrated strong rhetorical unity among the 28 members, but debuted a limited package of reassurance measures for NATO's eastern allies. Allies agreed to a Readiness Action Plan, which will create a rapidly deployable 4,000-troop task force to spearhead NATO's response force, in addition to an enhanced regional exercise and training program. This reassurance package also augments the presence of 600 U.S. soldiers in the Baltic States and Poland, enhanced NATO air policing, and the readiness of NATO's Multinational Corps–Northeast Regional Headquarters in Szczecin, Poland.

Unfortunately, NATO allies were only able to agree to a "persistent" rotational force presence in the east and not a permanent deployment. The current formula of "persistent rotations" conveys a message to Russia that the crisis along NATO's border is a temporary phenomenon rather than a new and long-term destabilizing force. The hoped-for deployment of NATO's 4,000-troop spearhead force stands in stark contrast to the continuous mobilization of tens of thousands of Russian forces along Ukraine's border over the past six months.

NATO allies have also not been able to outline a new, overarching deterrence doctrine against hybrid warfare tactics. For example, in Eastern Ukraine Russia has deployed special force units disguised as separatist militants; utilized information, cyber, energy, and trade warfare tactics; and agitated ethnic Russian communities in order to achieve its aims. NATO remains underprepared to confront such unconventional challenges. Although NATO has created–or will shortly–Centers of Excellence in cyber warfare, energy security, and strategic communications in an attempt to address specific elements of hybrid warfare by enhancing policies and awareness (not surprisingly each of these centers resides in a Baltic State), the alliance has yet to make any decisive changes.

As NATO confronts and attempts to deter the long-term security implications of "Novorossiya," the Alliance will continue to rally around transatlantic unity and solidarity, as well as the shared commitment to uphold Article 5 treaty obligations. As Russia continues to further test NATO's resolve in and around its territory, the Alliance must develop a new and flexible deterrence strategy against hybrid warfare that permanently stations NATO forces in the East, in addition to the readily available rapid-reaction forces. To implement this strategy, NATO should consider deploying at least one heavy brigade combat team (BCT)-sized deployment to the region with a mix of U.S. and European NATO troops. Likewise, the Szczecin HQ in western Poland could be substantially augmented with more senior leadership and staffed with more NATO personnel.

Against the backdrop of Russia's invasion of Georgia in 2008, its seizure of Crimea, and its encroachment into Ukraine, NATO must translate its powerful rhetoric into a tangible military presence. NATO must overcome its hesitancy, if not outright opposition, to the permanent stationing of NATO troops in the region—most notably those objections articulated by Berlin. As NATO prepares to deter hybrid warfare, it must also retain deterrence capabilities against a potential direct threat by Russia against NATO's eastern flank. By developing a robust deterrent posture built on a permanent troop and asset deployment along the frontier, combined with transatlantic unity, Moscow will be unable to erode confidence in NATO's Article 5 commitment to its eastern members. Failure to do so will call into question NATO's viability when Russia decides to probe a NATO member in an attempt to expose the lack of Alliance resolve. The political framework for implementing such a deterrent strategy has already been established in the outlines of President Obama's recent speeches and statements in Warsaw and Tallinn, and reinforced by remarks from European leaders and the new NATO Secretary General Jens Stoltenberg.

Without a sufficient NATO deterrent policy, NATO's hesitancy will further embolden Russia to exert pressure along NATO's periphery. At present,

NATO's response has been to focus on de-escalation rather than deterrence. Hence, efforts to seek political accommodation and compromise have hobbled a larger strategic deterrent redesign that is imperative if NATO is to remain a credible alliance.

PART III

How Can the United States Best Exert Influence in Today's Middle East?

15. ACTING AND REACTING IN THE MIDDLE EAST

Jon B. Alterman

When mass protests broke out in the Arab world in 2011, the Obama administration saw opportunity. The president helped push long-time U.S. ally Hosni Mubarak to step down from the Egyptian presidency, noting, "I think history will end up recording that at every juncture in the situation in Egypt that we were on the right side of history."

Almost four years later, "people power" has not taken hold in the Middle East. Some countries, such as Libya and Syria, hemorrhage from civil wars that started as peaceful protests. In Egypt, elections produced a government so exclusionary that after a year in power, much of the public supported a return to military rule. Three and a half years after the death of Osama bin Laden, jihadis are resurgent in the region. Meanwhile, the United States finds itself fighting battles in the Middle East with strained alliances and diminished influence. What went wrong?

Where one stands depends on where one sits. For some, the problem is that the United States swiftly abandoned principles for expediency. Speaking at the State Department a week after bin Laden's death, the president raised idealists' hopes, favorably comparing protests in the Middle East to the American Revolution and the U.S. struggle for civil rights in the 1950s and 1960s. "After decades of accepting the world as it is in the region," he said, "we have a chance to pursue the world as it should be." And yet, the rise of violence and disorder in the Middle East pushed the United States to work more closely with the militaries, intelligence services, and authoritarian leaders who only months before seemed anachronistic.

The tension between ideals and interests has been starkly clear in Bahrain, where the U.S. Fifth Fleet has its headquarters, and where a Sunni-led government, with support from Saudi Arabia and other neighbors, has been suppressing an uprising by the Shi'a majority. Naval base operations have not been affected, and the United States resumed sales of some military equipment only months after the unrest began.

For others, however, the United States has remained not only idealistic but naïve in the face of real and persistent threats in the Middle East. Gulf Arab allies continue to complain that the Obama administration "threw Hosni Mubarak under the bus," yielding to chaos. Conservative regional governments express puzzlement that the United States has remained blind to the menace of the Muslim Brotherhood, seeing democrats where these governments saw power-hungry theocrats. These governments not only wonder about U.S. support should they face internal challenges, but even if the United States would provide aid and comfort to their enemies out of a misplaced belief in the enemies' good intentions. Realists in the United States complain that the disorder that accompanies rapid political change is both predictable and profound, and the eagerness with which the United States embraced such change reflects a lack of historical awareness or strategic thinking.

Perhaps most surprising in recent months, in the arenas where the United States has been putting forth the greatest effort—in Iraq, for example—the U.S. government has put the emphasis squarely on government-to-government relationships. In so doing, the president is relying on often-ineffective or corrupt officials to reach the large and dissatisfied populations in whom the president had seen such promise a few years before.

While some rush to ascribe incompetence or even malice to U.S. government actions, the lack of effectiveness is instead a product of sustained U.S. uncertainty. Tumultuous politics in the Middle East have pushed the United States toward a more circumspect attitude toward the permanence of its allies. Put simply, it is not willing to bet on their success. The speed with which the United States moved to establish a working relationship with the Muslim Brotherhood in Egypt was chilling to many regional leaders, as was the slow reluctance with which the United States accepted the Egyptian army's seizing power. For the United States, the episode was a principled expression of concentrating on process rather than outcome. For Arab allies, it was an opportunistic embrace of victors over friends.

Distrust of U.S. intentions colors Arab leaders' assessment of U.S.-led negotiations over the Iranian nuclear program. Arab governments fear that the United States will try too hard to accommodate Iran in the negotiations and react too passively to subsequent Iranian violations of its agreements, leaving them enveloped by Iranian hegemonic ambitions. The fears of Gulf leaders in particular are abetted by the prospect of U.S. energy independence, which they see as diminishing U.S. interest in their partnership, and in their security.

While there is widespread agreement that U.S. policy in the Middle East should be responsive to conditions on the ground, there is widespread concern that it has become wholly reactive—crisis-driven, unprincipled, and uncoordinated. The perception that it is reactive elicits complaints that it is not reactive enough to an individual petitioner's complaints. That makes it appear feckless as well.

Whether one considers the "Transformational Diplomacy" of Condoleezza Rice or the "21st-Century Statecraft" of Hillary Clinton, the United States continues to lack a strategy it needs for an increasingly complex world—and increasingly complex Middle East—in which non-state actors are stronger, communications are more robust, and priorities harder to sustain. Equally importantly, foreign policy complexity has helped create a world in which U.S. strategic priorities are increasingly hard to discern. This is especially so given a strong bureaucratic impulse toward the inclusion of priorities in strategic documents rather than choosing between them.

A clearer strategy would look like this: global energy security—broadly defined—is certainly in the strategic interest of the United States, as is containing transnational terrorism. So too is preserving the security of key allies against hostile states, and enhancing the resilience of friendly governments. Working with friendly states in the region, in Europe, and in Asia, those should be the strategic goals. In order to pursue them, the United States should not only work with friendly governments, but also push to empower a range of like-minded non-state actors, in the United States and abroad. Through it all, the United States must keep in mind that some of its greatest successes have come not from what it has done directly, but through creating institutions and incentives that encourage people and governments to act in desirable ways. The United States still needs to react, but those reactions need to be a smaller share of its actions in the Middle East and beyond.

16. THE NEED FOR BETTER CIVIL-MILITARY PLANNING

Anthony H. Cordesman

The United States is now more than a decade into wars attempting to bring security and stability to the Middle East. The results have not been good. The initial U.S. military victory in Iraq that overthrew Saddam Hussein was followed by eight years of irregular warfare, a pause, and now a new war against ISIS. The U.S. military effort to lead from behind in Libya after 2011 has left instability bordering on chaos in that country. The U.S. military effort in Yemen has not prevented its capital and government from falling to Houthi rebels.

The U.S. invasion of Iraq in 2003 had the unintended consequence of totally destabilizing the military balance in the Gulf by destroying Iraq's military forces, and contributing to a massive regional arms race between Iran and the United States and Iran's Arab neighbors. The broader upheavals in the Arab world have offset any other gains in the war in terrorism. The Study of Terrorism and Response to Terrorism (START) global database on terrorism shows an increase from fewer than 300 major incidents a year in the Middle East and North Africa (MENA) region during 1998 to 2004, to 1,600 in 2008, then from 1,500 in 2010 to 1,700 in 2011, 2,500 in 2012, and 4,650 in 2013—a fifteenfold increase since 2002, and threefold increase since 2010.

A recent RAND study found that the number of Salafi jihadists more than doubled from 2010 to 2013, according to both low and high estimates. The war in Syria was the single most important attraction for Salafi-jihadist fighters. There was a significant increase in attacks by al Qaeda-affiliated groups between 2007 and 2013, with most of the violence in 2013 perpetrated by ISIS (43 percent), which eventually left al Qaeda; al Shabaab (25 percent); Jabhat al-Nusra (21 percent); and al Qaeda in the Arabian Peninsula (10 percent).

The United States cannot ignore the need to meet real threats with military force, or the need to create effective counterterrorism programs. It also, however, urgently needs to look at the almost complete failure to create effective civil-military plans and programs during both the Afghan and Iraq wars, the critical failures to manage them effectively and establish transparency, adequate fiscal controls, and measures of effectiveness. By Congressional Research Service (CRS) estimates, the United States has already spent some $1.8 trillion on the two wars, and both SIGIR (Special Inspector General for Iraq Reconstruction) and SIGAR (Special Inspector General for Afghanistan Reconstruction) have shown the military and civil aid aspects of this spending involved incredible amounts of waste, fraud, and corruption.

The weakest links lay in the civilian side of aid spending, and in the poor planning, weak management, and lack of proper audits and measures of effectiveness by the State Department and U.S. Agency for International Development (USAID). There is clear need for a comprehensive review of the reason for these failures and to find ways to create a structure that can cope with these challenges in the future. As the new war against ISIS makes clear, no war against jihadism, terrorism, or an extremist sanctuary can ever be won by force alone.

Here, Americans and Europeans need to understand that the primary threat is not to outside states, and that, as RAND states, "Approximately 99 percent of the attacks by al Qaeda and its affiliates in 2013 were against 'near enemy' targets in North Africa, the Middle East, and other regions outside of the West, the highest percentage of attacks against the near enemy in our database."

As the UN Arab Human Development Reports have made clear since 2002, however, both outsiders and MENA states need to pay far more attention to the causes of these civil problems. They are complex, they vary by country, and analysts disagree about the importance of given issues, but even a short list of key pressures shows why extremism, violence, and instability will continue indefinitely unless their civil causes are properly addressed.

The MENA region is largely a desert with declining aquifers, river flow, and rain, and dependence on finite amounts of fossil water. It is also under incredible demographic pressure. According to the U.S. Census Bureau, the total population for the MENA region was about 83 million in 1950. In 2014 the population was 404 million—roughly five times higher. Its rate of growth is decreasing, but conservative estimates put its population at 590 million in 2050—seven times higher than in 1950—and 46 percent higher than in 2014.

Part of the reason is aging. Life expectancy increased by roughly 12 years, from approximately 61 years to 73 years, on an average after 1900. At the same time, the dependency ratio—the number of people who depend on others for income—increased because so much of the population was so young. The CIA Factbook estimates that the percentage of citizens 14 years of age or younger is 28–38 percent in most MENA countries. For comparison, they are 19.4 percent in the United States, 13.8 percent in Italy, and 13.2 percent in Japan.

This creates immense pressure on young people in countries that have not invested properly in education, where governments have failed to create meaningful jobs and careers commensurate with the increase in population. Compounding the problem, in many societies women are not allowed to compete or be productive. In many cases, disguised unemployment leaves only dead-end jobs that do not cover basic family costs, including marriage, children, or housing. These problems are more destabilizing than direct unemployment, particularly in countries that have failed to modernize and reform their economies and lack major oil wealth.

Many MENA citizens have also been forced to leave the areas that provided them their sect, ethnicity, and tribe with a traditional social safety net. There has been a drop, not an increase, in arable land, and the emerging market structures for agriculture create strong pressure to invest capital in agriculture and reduce the number of people on the land.

This push away from the land, and sheer demographic pressure, are leading in all but the richest oil exporters to the unstable hyper-urbanization of formerly rural societies. To make matters worse, governments are not keeping up with matching development, housing, infrastructure, or investment in education, and sometimes fail to provide the most basic essentials, such as water and electricity. The modernization of the wealthier part of most MENA cities disguises large slums, low income, and long commutes. As a rough estimate, nations with 16–18 percent urbanization in 1950 are now well over 40 percent today.

The CIA estimates the rate of urbanization in Qatar is 98 percent, 73 percent in Algeria, 82.3 percent in Saudi Arabia, and 82.7 percent in Jordan. In many cases, this creates new pressures that also increase sectarian, ethnic, and tribal tensions. It is also made much worse by the increasing flow of refugees and internal displaced persons coming from local and international conflicts—Algeria's past civil war, the Iran-Iraq War and conflicts in Iraq, Arab-Palestinian conflicts, and ongoing civil wars in Libya, Syria, and Yemen.

If one looks at national budgets and UN data, many non-oil countries—and several key oil countries like Algeria, Libya, Iran, and Iraq—do not invest in their civil sector proportionately to the rise in their population and fall badly behind in spending on education and social services. A major shortfall now exists between required levels of education in years and actual schooling. UN estimates indicate that the average required schooling totals 10.6 years in the MENA area, but that the mean average of actual years is 6. This is not bad by South Asian and African standards, but it compares with 10.4 years in Europe, and far too often it creates alienated young men who learn about

Islam by rote memorization, are open to extremists, and have no reason to be loyal to their regimes.

Secularism and existing political structures are often weak. The ideologies of the past have all failed, and the indices of the World Bank and Transparency International show high levels of corruption, high levels of violence, chronic failures of effective economic reform, and poor rule of law. A combination of authoritarianism, corruption, lack of transparency, and faulty rule of law helps ensure that there are no real political parties and no opposition leaders really capable of governance. In turn, the opposition often becomes covert and ideological, extreme, and violent. State Department Human Rights Reports also warn that justice systems are often repressive and dysfunctional in civil and criminal areas, and religious extremism acquires political legitimacy by default—particularly since religious extremists seem to do the best job of exploiting the internet, religious societies, and social networks.

Some MENA states still do well and modernize and reform, but there is an immense disparity of income between and within MENA nations. The CIA estimates that GDP per capita is $2,500 in Yemen, $6,000 in Jordan, $6,600 in Egypt, $7,000 in Algeria, $7,100 in Iraq, $12,800 in Iran, $31,300 in Saudi Arabia, and $102,100 in Qatar—this compares with $52,800 in the United States. If one looks at gross national income (GNI) per capita, the average was $8,317 in 2013 for the Arab world versus $33,391 for very high development countries. Moreover, corruption and favoritism skew the numbers in favor of the elite, and keep power in the hands of those with strong ethnic, sectarian, and tribal biases.

As some of these figures show, one also needs to be very cautious in talking about MENA "oil wealth." Some Gulf monarchies do well, but the Department of Energy/Energy Information Administration (DOE/EIA) estimates that per capita oil wealth in Organization of the Petroleum Exporting Countries (OPEC) states ranges from only $1,667 in Algeria to $2,706 in Iraq, $8,939 in Saudi Arabia, and $40,943 in Qatar. Distribution can range from reasonable to terrible, and the "Dutch disease" is a hiccup compared to the problems oil revenues create in the MENA area.

This expansive set of factors helps explain why U.S. commanders, policy planners, and intelligence experts talk about a decade—or decades—of unrest, and warn again and again that every military victory or counterterrorism strike has marginal effect. Counterterrorism, counterinsurgency, and winning open conflict are not going to do the job. Unless the United States can do a far better job of addressing the civilian side of such conflicts, and broaden the nature of its efforts to create effective civil and military partnerships, every "victory" will be no more real than the moment Sisyphus got the rock near the peak.

17. THE CHALLENGE OF NON-STATE ACTORS

Haim Malka

After half a century during which the Middle East was divided along Cold War lines between U.S. allies and adversaries, the United States now has friendly relations with nearly every Arab state, save the Assad regime in Syria. Yet, non-state armed groups have emerged as key protagonists in conflicts around the region, and they are often hostile to the United States. Today they undermine U.S. policy goals, destabilize fragile states, and kill civilians.

More than ever before, the United States must address a mutating set of foes that operates in increasingly complex political environments. Doing so will require U.S. government officials to demonstrate vigilance, dynamism, and creativity at a time when security concerns push many to huddle inside embassy walls.

The United States has many fewer tools to influence non-state armed groups than it has with governments—and close bilateral ties with governments have encouraged the United States to designate many such groups as foreign terrorist organizations, complicating any U.S. government contact with them at all. When it comes to non-state armed groups, the tools and the objective have often been limited to "isolate" or "eliminate."

And yet, these groups have flourished. Throughout the Middle East, non-state armed groups have adapted to shifting political constraints and opportunities, and they have increasingly adopted characteristics of states. Such groups control territory, engage in diplomacy, build constituencies, and play politics. Rather than merely looking for a stake in existing state systems, non-state groups are reinventing those systems.

Part of the challenge for the United States is how to address the root causes of support that these armed groups enjoy. In many cases, non-state armed groups are inherently political actors with highly refined objectives that resonate with significant parts of local populations. Hezbollah fought for the rights of the Shi'a majority population that had long been marginalized in modern Lebanon. Hamas presented an Islamist alternative to the Palestine Liberation Organization's (PLO) arrogance and corruption, which critics believed had done little to establish an independent Palestinian state. Even in the fight against al Qaeda and ISIS, there seems to be a steady supply of young men willing to die for the ideology and goals these movements espouse. While U.S. rhetoric describes ISIS in polemical terms, the reality is that ISIS has two powerful drivers of support: it is a utopian social and political entity that appeals to disaffected young people, and it is a powerful protector of sectarian interests for millions of Sunni Arabs in Syria and Iraq who feel systematically disenfranchised.

The group will continue attracting foreigners as long as it convinces them that its project to build the caliphate remains sincere and a viable alternative to other forms of government in the region; it will likely continue finding support in Iraq as long as many under their rule believe that Shi'a politicians remain a larger threat to their interests.

Beyond their political acumen, many non-state armed groups have become security providers. Islamist military brigades went on the Libyan government payroll after the revolution and provided security at hospitals and government installations. Hamas, though it remains committed to fighting Israel, has at times prevented rocket fire by smaller militant groups and, through its security monopoly, limited the activities of al Qaeda-affiliated cells in Gaza that could pose a more lethal threat. In Syria, Hezbollah is fighting ISIS and the al Qaeda affiliated

Jabhat al-Nusra, a goal that overlaps with that of the United States.

It is these groups' political dimension, then, that poses the most complex challenges for U.S. policymakers. The experiences of the last several decades suggest that non-state armed groups cannot be eliminated. They can be contained, their capabilities can be degraded, but by their nature they continue to evolve: they adjust to new constraints, exploit opportunities, and reinvent themselves to meet new environments.

For the United States, victory is unlikely to be found through defeating and eliminating these groups. Instead, the United States must work to change the political and social conditions that allow them to thrive. How to develop state structures that meet the needs of populations and offer a vision for them will be the great challenge for the next generation in the Middle East. If governments don't take the lead in putting forward new visions that resonate with their populations, non-state armed groups will do it for them.

18. COUNTERTERRORISM SUCCESS AND FAILINGS

Samuel J. Brannen

A s President Obama oversees military operations against ISIS, he and his advisers should also be sure to focus on the effectiveness of military operations against terrorist groups over the past 13 years. While succeeding in the short term—largely keeping the United States and its citizens safe from attack—U.S.-led strikes have neither stopped the spread of Islamist extremism, nor addressed growing, related state-level instability from Pakistan to Nigeria.

The increasing capability of terrorists to destroy people and property and to command attention is presenting itself as the strategic challenge of a generation. In response to the most pressing threats, the United States has carried out a series of military strikes, sometimes directly and sometimes through allied militaries, sometimes on the ground and sometimes from the air. Military action against ISIS is the latest U.S. campaign against an armed terrorist group operating from a weak state.

Addressing the long-term challenge of ISIS must begin with broad understanding of the utility of military force against this enemy—the most visible, costly, and active element of U.S. strategy to date. It is true that through innovation, investment, grit, and sacrifice across the U.S. national security enterprise, the United States has developed a remarkable capability to detect and disrupt terrorist plots emanating from overseas. Unmanned aerial systems can operate over remote geographies without putting a single American in harm's way, while Special Forces capture or kill high-value leaders deep inside sovereign countries, with or without diplomatic permission. The enemy is nowhere safe, and largely the U.S. intelligence community can provide strategic (if not always tactical) warning of an adversary's activities.

Yet, there are firm limits on what strategic results this approach to counterterrorism brings. Secretary of Defense Chuck Hagel told the House Armed Services Committee in September 2014 that "American military power alone cannot eradicate the threats posed by ISIS to the United States, our allies and our friends and partners in the region." Despite remarkable operational successes in a global direct action campaign by the U.S. intelligence community and the military, a growing web of terrorist groups continues to attract and train recruits, regrow leaders, maintain funding, and gain new operational footholds. Osama bin Laden and hundreds of his top lieutenants and adherents are captured or dead, but during the past decade terrorist groups have expanded across the Middle East and North Africa. As these groups metastasize, U.S. military assets have been spread thin. The U.S. military maintains unflinching focus on counterterrorism at the expense of other difficult security challenges and strategic imperatives that will matter in years and decades to come.

Former Secretary of Defense Bob Gates has observed that the incredible capability of the U.S. military can be a liability: "Our foreign and national security policy has become too militarized, the use of force too easy for presidents." With so much military capability on call for the president, and the broad counterterrorism authorities endowed in presidential findings and the 2001 Authorization for Use of Military Force, there is a distortion in the cost-benefit analysis for action versus inaction (or less direct approaches). When option A is to attack the terrorist network and option B is essentially to do nothing, the choice is not difficult, even if it is admittedly short term.

But often, the choice to use military force empowers this enemy. Former Secretary of Defense Donald Rumsfeld asked his staff in an October 2003 memo, "Are we capturing, killing or deterring and dissuading more terrorists every day than the madrassas and the radical clerics are recruiting, training and deploying against us?" The answer to that question is as unnerving today as when he asked it. Al Qaeda and ISIS not only do not seem to mind that they are hunted; they seem to thrive because of it. Their propaganda depends on images of battle against a superior adversary, stoking a sense of victimization and injustice. Israel has experienced a similar phenomenon in its successive campaigns against Hezbollah and Hamas: battlefield victories translate at best into stalemate and at worst into political losses in a regional context. Terrorist groups feed on the instability and economic decimation that warfare brings.

A more effective U.S. counterterrorism approach is straightforward, well understood, and yet has proven elusive to two administrations. It would be far better to balance the use of military force in the short term against adversaries directly threatening the interests of the United States and its allies and partners with the need to pursue other approaches that cut off recruits and support for these groups in the medium and long terms.

Over the past 13 years, in addition to its military successes the United States has improved border and transportation security, and developed powerful counter-threat finance tools. But it has fallen markedly short in other key areas. The good news is that the shortfalls and needed capabilities are well understood. They are mainly in the areas of information operations, partner security forces and law enforcement capacity building, economic and political development in weak states, and human rights. Our failure to make successful investments in these areas in Iraq helps explain the current challenges the United States and its allies—including the Iraqi government—face there now.

Progress on these issues will require sustained attention from the president and his top advisers. The National Security Council must give the same attention to building up and exercising these tools as it does direct-action counterterrorism. Congress must similarly lend its attention to the necessary missing ingredients of a better approach to counterterrorism. Military force is a sometimes necessary, but strategically insufficient, answer to a growing threat.

PART IV

Is the Rebalance to Asia Sustainable?

19. ASIAN PERCEPTIONS OF THE REBALANCE

Michael J. Green and Zack Cooper

Three years have passed since President Barack Obama announced the U.S. "rebalance" to Asia. A recent CSIS survey found that 79 percent of strategic elites in Asia support the rebalance, with opposition mainly coming from China where only 23 percent were in support. Yet, as enthusiastic as most Asian observers are about a renewed U.S. focus on their region, the rebalance or "pivot" to Asia has been overshadowed by doubts regarding the administration's ability to follow through. In the CSIS survey, 51 percent of elites questioned whether the rebalance has been effectively resourced or implemented. Concerns center on three questions.

First, can the administration and the Congress reach agreement on the Trans-Pacific Partnership (TPP)? At present, the core of the negotiations between Japan and the United States have broken down over about five remaining issues, with Washington blaming Japanese intransigence and Tokyo blaming the Obama administration's unwillingness to seek Congressional Trade Promotion Authority (TPA). TPP is seen in the region as an indispensable cornerstone for building an open and inclusive trans-Pacific economic architecture going forward.

Second, does the United States have the willpower to counter increasing evidence of coercion in the region? Chinese mercantile and paramilitary coercion against claimant states in the

East and South China Seas and North Korea's ongoing nuclear weapons and missile programs have caused regional allies and partners to carefully watch the U.S. defense budget and the U.S. responses to the crises in Syria, Iraq, and Ukraine. On the one hand, they worry that renewed U.S. involvement in the Middle East or Europe will undercut the rebalance to Asia; but on the other hand, they worry about Washington's lack of demonstrated resolve in these cases and the signal this sends for Asia.

Third, what is the administration's bottom line in Asia? Is the objective of the rebalance a "new model of great power relations" with China—as the administration has announced at various points, to the chagrin of allies and partners like Japan or India that are relegated to non-great power status by Beijing? Or is the objective to strengthen security and economic partnerships with states under pressure from China, which Beijing views as a new form of containment? The success of the rebalance depends in large measure on how credibly and consistently the United States articulates its own role in shaping a future regional order.

While these questions percolate around the U.S. rebalance, there is good news for the administration as it refocuses on Asia and the Pacific over the coming years. First, elites in Asia appear to have confidence in American leadership overall, with 57 percent of respondents to the 2014 CSIS survey predicting that among various scenarios for the future of Asian order a decade from now, continued U.S. leadership was most likely. The major powers, including China, were most certain of this future. As President Obama prepares to travel in November to the East Asia Summit (EAS) and Asia-Pacific Economic Cooperation (APEC) summit, the administration would do well to use the opportunity to better define its vision for the rebalance in the years ahead.

20. KEEPING FOCUS ON KOREA
Victor Cha

It is hard to tell what the bigger concern on the Korean peninsu-la will be over the next year: more nuclear weapons and ballistic missile tests by the North, or potential political discontinuities inside the Pyongyang regime. Neither is a good outcome.

The first scenario would highlight the fact that over 20 years after the first nuclear agreement with North Korea in October 1994 (the Agreed Framework), and 10 years after the second nu-clear agreement in September 2005 (the Six-Party Joint State-ment), the problem has become exponentially worse in 2015. North Korea, under Kim Jong-un's byongjin strategy appears to be aiming to develop the full spectrum of nuclear capabilities, from plutonium and uranium-based weapons to potential bat-tlefield use. The Obama administration might try to make one last push for a denuclearization deal like the September 2005 agreement, but success would be highly unlikely.

The second scenario is no better. The machinations of North Korean leadership dynamics raise concerns about regime sta-bility. It is not clear if the young leader is calling the shots or if there are power struggles among elites in the party and military over a shrinking pie. Even if internal power struggles are not the problem, Kim's health may be. Westerners who have met the young leader in person at diplomatic functions in Pyongyang have observed that he is grossly obese, much more so than official pictures depict; that he is a chain smoker; that he drinks heavily;

and that his face looks unusually unhealthy for a 29- or 30-year-old. There is a history of heart disease in the family (Kim's father and grandfather both died of massive heart attacks), as well as purported kidney and liver problems. The chances that he can rule for decades like his predecessors are slim.

The challenge for the United States will be how to maintain focus on this problem when the White House will be preoccupied with Ebola in West Africa, Russia and Ukraine, and the war against ISIS. A crisis with the North (in the form of a fourth nuclear test or provocations against South Korea) will certainly grab attention, but the reaction will be to seek a temporary solution that provides compensation to Pyongyang in return for de-escalation—a familiar outcome that has contributed directly to the growth of the North's nuclear program over the past 25 years. On the other hand, if the North does not invoke a crisis it will mean little attention from Washington, allowing the North's nuclear program to develop unimpeded.

The best antidote to this catch-22 is to continue robust defense cooperation with South Korea. This means enhancing missile defense, including the introduction of Terminal High Altitude Area Defense (THAAD) to the peninsula; delay of the transfer of wartime operational control (OPCON) from the United States to South Korea; and a rigorous regimen of military exercises to reinforce deterrence. Washington and Seoul might consider improved defense cooperation in areas like drone technology, which could be useful against North Korea. Regional security also requires better defense cooperation and information sharing between South Korea and Japan. As reluctant as the South Koreans may be to work with their neighbor, enhanced U.S.-Japan-Korea trilateral alliance cooperation is the best answer to North Korea's threats and possible regime instability.

North Korea is not the only issue on the U.S.-Republic of Korea (ROK) security agenda in 2015. Look for the two allies to complete a new civilian nuclear energy agreement that will form the basis of a new era of safe and proliferation-free nuclear cooperation. Washington and Seoul are likely to put flesh on the bones of a development assistance agreement made between the two Peace Corps last year (South Korea has the world's second-largest Peace Corps next to the United States) and on health security initiatives. These types of projects reinforce the alliance's growing scope not only to operate on the peninsula but also to provide public goods for the broader world community. Should the Trans-Pacific Partnership be completed in 2015, also look for South Korea to be one of the first major economies to seek membership in the institution.

Despite the strong ties between ROK president Park Guen-hye and Chinese leader Xi Jinping, 2015 may be a year in which we see this deepening relationship put to the test. North Korean provocations will raise expectations in Seoul that Beijing should act expeditiously in punishing the North. Meanwhile, China is likely to call in some chips with the ROK by lobbying against the introduction of THAAD to the peninsula. Neither "ask" is likely to be heeded by the other side, which will create mutual disappointment.

21. ECONOMIC IMPERATIVE IN SOUTHEAST ASIA

Ernest Z. Bower

While there is a wide range of differing perceptions about the U.S. rebalance in Southeast Asia, there is a regional consensus that a strong, sustainable U.S. presence is necessary to retain regional peace and stability, which are in turn prerequisites for economic growth.

To build an effective strategy to promote its interests in the region, the United States needs to digest the fact that in Asia, economics are the foundation for security. In other words, any U.S. security and military strategy for Asia will be incomplete and ineffective without a comprehensive economic thrust. Current U.S. economic offerings are insufficient because they don't include all of the key countries. Nor do they articulate a comprehensive goal that makes sense to Americans seeking new jobs as well as Asian partners seeking expanded investment, trade, and the benefits U.S. companies bring, including training, education, and investment in communities and infrastructure.

A number of factors are driving Southeast Asia to send the United States a strong demand signal for engagement:

- Anxiety over China's rapid economic growth and its demonstrated willingness to use economic leverage to force neighbors to conform with its demands in disputes;

- China's rapid increase in military capability;

- Admiration for elements of what the United States stands for, including democracy, freedom, and human rights;

- A well-developed instinct for geopolitical balancing.

President Obama's administration deserves credit for saying and doing many of the right things in this context, including sustaining a strong bipartisan continuity of focus on Asia. His team has articulated an Association of Southeast Asian Nations (ASEAN)-focused strategic outlook that sees the new geopolitical center of gravity as the point where the Indian and Pacific oceans meet, namely in Indonesia, ASEAN's anchor. Former Secretary of State Hillary Clinton described ASEAN as the "fulcrum" of evolving security and economic architecture in Asia.

Function has followed form, for the most part. President Obama successfully engaged ASEAN by acceding to the group's Treaty of Amity and Cooperation, joining the East Asia Summit, and establishing diplomatic relations with a reforming Myanmar. Obama's secretaries of state have not missed an ASEAN Regional Forum; his secretaries of defense have forged ahead with the ASEAN Defense Ministers' Meeting-Plus and held a U.S.-ASEAN Defense Forum that the United States hopes to repeat annually. The president himself elevated his annual meeting with the 10 ASEAN leaders to a summit, thereby institutionalizing the high-level engagement.

Additionally, steps have been taken to deepen bilateral ties with allies and important partners. The Enhanced Defense Cooperation Agreement was negotiated in the Philippines, four littoral combat ships now have a home in Singapore, military-to-military ties with Indonesia have been normalized, and the embargo on lethal weapons sales to Vietnam has been partially lifted. These steps, in addition to concentrated efforts to establish comprehensive or strategic partnerships with other ASEAN countries, are foundational benchmarks.

These steps are necessary, but not sufficient. Southeast Asia worries about Beijing's perception that Washington won't sustain this level of focus and investment in Asia generally and Southeast Asia in particular. Most ASEAN members believe that Beijing has committed to achieving regional leadership by the Chinese Communist Party's 100th birthday in 2021 and regional hegemony by the People's Republic of China's centennial in 2049. ASEAN's members see China incrementally testing U.S. resolve, pushing Beijing's goals to dominate the first and second island chain in the near- to midterm. China is testing the limits of its new power, and trying to understand where lines will be drawn.

This creates a dilemma for most Southeast Asian countries. ASEAN needs China to be secure, economically successful, and active in economic integration, but it does not want to be dominated by China. Nor do any Southeast Asia countries want to emulate Chinese values or governance systems, including Vietnam. This conundrum is well demonstrated by the recent debate around China's campaign to develop a new set of Sino-centric institutions to supplant, or at least regionally augment, existing entities. A good example is the proposed Asian Infrastructure Investment Bank. ASEAN countries badly need more infrastructure investment and feel current mechanisms such as the World Bank, the Asian Development Bank, and the global private sector are not acting quickly enough. But they worry a great deal about giving Beijing more economic leverage.

To complete the rebalance in Southeast Asia, the United States needs presidential leadership to build a political foundation for future engagement in Asia. President Obama needs to talk to Americans himself, in the United States, about why Asia is fundamentally important to U.S. prosperity and peace. This above all other actions will convince Asia that the United States is committed for the long term. This leadership effort cannot be deputized or delegated, though the ground work has certainly been laid in speeches by successive Obama national security advisers and other key cabinet members.

Asia wonders why talking about foreign policy, trade, and Asia is seen as a negative in the context of U.S. domestic politics. Asian partners are being told repeatedly that the White House will spend political capital on the Trans-Pacific Partnership after the November midterm elections. This is not a good message in Asia. It undercuts a belief in a sustainable and serious

U.S. commitment to the region. Engagement in Asia cannot and should not be something the administration squeezes in during the lame-duck session or after elections so it doesn't divide its political base. The United States must develop an Asia consensus that serves as a foundation for policymaking for the remainder of the 21st century and beyond.

22. THE LONG VIEW ON INDIA

Richard M. Rossow

Ironically, the U.S. rebalance to Asia is viewed by some in India as a pivot away from their country. Repeated U.S. attempts to initiate top-down cooperation in strategic sectors, such as civilian nuclear power and defense trade, have experienced uneven success. Today, some senior U.S. policymakers privately question efforts to court a nation that often appears unwilling to reciprocate U.S. outreach. Few would argue that, in 20 years, a rising India will not play an important role in regional stability. For the United States to be a partner in this future, it must commit to finding small ways to work toward this vision—even if there will be few instances of short-term gratification.

U.S. policymakers have a powerful predilection toward tangible deliverables. Senior officials want to walk away from public service with a sense that they, as individuals, made some particular contribution to America's strategic success. There is less interest in engaging in relationships where there are low expectations for immediate repayment. Unfortunately, India has fallen into this category.

President George W. Bush placed a "big bet" on India as a distinctly important partner in Asia's future. But with the rebalance, India sees the United States as placing multiple smaller bets across Asia, with little strategic focus on India. The truth, of course, is much more nuanced; defense relations are expanding and space cooperation is back on the agenda, while nuclear cooperation is stuck in neutral largely due to India's inability to open the door for commercial trade.

The Bharatiya Janata Party's (BJP) resounding victory in the spring 2014 parliamentary election offers a chance to review how the United States and India might engage on strategic affairs. This BJP government is not the Congress Party, and therefore historical positions concerning nonalignment bear less significance. While there will still be adherents to nonalignment in the bureaucracy, policymakers will be willing to approach issues differently. While India has no desire to be seen as a junior partner to Washington, Narendra Modi's government is more open to expanding cooperation with the United States on a whole range of global issues.

There are already strong signals that New Delhi is thinking differently about its global interests, as evidenced by the Joint Statement issued following Prime Minister Modi's September 2014 visit to Washington, D.C. While the statement rehashes and updates some of the areas previously highlighted for bilateral cooperation, it expands the number of areas where the United States and India promise to collaborate, including North Korea, Iraq, Syria, and the South China Sea. Historically, India has avoided being this specific when it comes to identifying regions where it has strategic concerns and interests.

If India is interested in being a partner to the United States in developing a new Asian security architecture, there are important domestic issues within India that must be addressed. First and foremost, finding a solution to the nuclear liability issue—which has thus far precluded American commercial involvement in India's nuclear power industry—must be tackled. Second, India must be more receptive to U.S. attempts to initiate co-development and co-production of next-generation defense equipment. Third, India must show more willingness to engage on trade. While trade and strategic issues are sometimes viewed through different lenses, many consider the Trans-Pacific Partnership free-trade agreement to be one of the more tangible initiatives of the rebalance. India's avoidance of engaging in high-standards trade agreements, combined with the Modi government's decision to walk away from the World Trade Organization's Trade Facilitation Agreement in July 2014, does not give confidence that the government is ready to make tough decisions on trade issues that could bind the United States and India closer together.

Building a comprehensive, strategic relationship with India will continue to be an elaborate courtship. The United States needs to sacrifice its fondness for regular, clear deliverables, and be prepared to play a long game that may take decades. But India must also show greater willingness to take decisions that form the building blocks of a deeper relationship. A thoughtful assessment of Asia in 20 years shows a convergence of interests, but there is much work to be done to make sure that the United States and India have a dependable and comfortable partnership.

23. MAINTAINING THE U.S.-JAPAN ALLIANCE

Nicholas Szechenyi

The U.S. rebalance to the Asia-Pacific region presents an opportunity to strengthen the U.S.-Japan alliance and further its role in maintaining regional security and prosperity. U.S. fiscal constraints and multiple crises in other parts of the world have prompted concern in Japan about the sustainability of the rebalance, but close ties with the United States are the cornerstone of Japanese foreign policy and the Abe government unveiled a national security strategy last year that mirrors U.S. diplomatic, economic, and security objectives in the region. There is much the two governments can do in the coming year to enhance alliance cooperation aimed at shaping the regional order.

Revised guidelines for bilateral defense cooperation expected by the end of 2014 will update the strategic framework for the alliance and signal a commitment to strengthen deterrence in an increasingly complex regional security environment. The two governments are conducting a policy dialogue to identify priorities. Examples listed in an interim report include maritime security; air and missile defense; intelligence, surveillance, and reconnaissance; capacity building; and space and cyber security. Core objectives are to increase Japan's defense capabilities and interoperability between the two militaries, and the Abe government's July 2014 decision to reinterpret the constitution and exercise the right of collective self-defense (or aid allies under attack) is potentially a means toward both ends. Requisite legislation for this policy reform will be submitted for parliamentary debate in 2015 and it will take some time to determine the impact in operational terms. Nonetheless, the guidelines likely will address the general implications for the alliance, which include improved information sharing as well as cooperation with other regional partners, a central tenet of the U.S. rebalance to Asia.

Japan will continue to seek U.S. support for its sovereignty claims over the Senkaku Islands and respond to the challenges posed by Chinese coercion in the East China Sea. Senior Obama administration officials have stated repeatedly that while the United States does not take a position on the islands' sovereignty, it does recognize Japan's administrative control over the islands and consequently Article V of the U.S.-Japan security treaty (which obligates the United States to defend Japan and all areas under its administrative control) applies. U.S. officials have also consistently voiced opposition to any unilateral attempts to coercively change the status quo, but declaratory policy alone will prove insufficient in deterring Chinese assertiveness. China has orchestrated multiple incursions into Japanese territorial waters and air space around the Senkaku Islands, probing activities that fall short of armed conflict but increase tension and instability. Japan would like to advance operational planning with the United States on these so-called gray zone contingencies and reduce the probability of accidental conflict. The guidelines revision process should facilitate such planning and the U.S. Pacific Command should shed any reticence about exploring cooperation in future gray zone scenarios.

A core pillar of Japan's national security strategy and the U.S. rebalance is economic power. In joining the Trans-Pacific Partnership trade negotiations, both countries have recognized that economic competitiveness and trade liberalization are inextricably linked. The United States and Japan, as the first- and third-largest economies in the world, respectively, are poised to fuel the economic engine that is the Asia Pacific and enhance their strategic influence by setting high standards for regional economic integration. Trade politics in both countries render the prospects for concluding TPP uncertain, but progress on the agreement in the year ahead will be critical to the credibility of Prime Minister Abe's structural reform agenda and the economic component of the U.S. rebalance. Article II of the U.S.-Japan security treaty focuses on economic cooperation, and joint leadership on TPP is a vital tool for enhancing both economic prosperity and security. Right now the United States and Japan are disagreeing on issues that probably account for less than 1 percent of our total bilateral trade. Both sides need to look to the larger strategic and economic picture. Japan should build on deregulation under way in the agricultural sector to sell TPP at home, and the White House needs to make the case politically not only for opening Japanese markets, but also to demonstrate to U.S. trading partners that President Obama is willing to fight for necessary Trade Promotion Authority (TPA) against opposition in his own party.

As a treaty ally of the United States, Japan naturally welcomes a sustained U.S. presence in the Asia-Pacific region and wants to be a partner in realizing the objectives of the rebalance. This is evidenced by an interest in expanding the parameters for bilateral security cooperation and setting standards for regional trade. Translating these shared strategic interests into action will prove important in terms of demonstrating Japan's leadership capacity and a sustained U.S. commitment to the region despite a plethora of foreign policy challenges elsewhere.

24. RECALIBRATING ON CHINA

Christopher K. Johnson

Sustaining the rebalance into 2015 will require crafting fresh approaches to managing the bilateral U.S.-China relationship while reassuring the region and encouraging Chinese leaders to understand Washington's abiding commitment to Asia without further exacerbating Chinese suspicions over U.S. intentions. On overall strategy, the administration needs to acknowledge more honestly that President Xi Jinping is not responding to the heavy dose of traditional U.S. messaging and cueing on maritime tensions and other security sore spots—or at least not in the way Washington would want. This does not require U.S. acquiescence to China's new policy tack, but it should give U.S. policymakers pause and a desire to reflect on whether—and how—U.S. actions may need to be recalibrated to deal with this dilemma.

At a more tactical level, the United States must not miss the opportunity afforded by the round of summits taking place in Asia in late 2014. China's tone has become noticeably less shrill, especially when it comes to relations with its regional neighbors. Whether it be Xi's successful trip to India or the steady—if still sub rosa—shift toward less antagonistic relations with Japan, it is obvious that Beijing is on at least a mini charm offensive. As a still relatively untested ruler on the world stage, President Xi is keen to show off his foreign policy acumen in playing host to all of the region's most important leaders at the APEC summit. Skillful U.S. diplomacy will seek to mold that instinct into an impetus for shaping the regional environment to sustain the warming trend in the coming year.

Above all, operationalizing such a strategy with China requires putting most of the administration's energy into advancing the economic and other nonsecurity elements of the rebalance. Given the seeming intractability of many of the security challenges in the relationship, emphasizing these other areas offers the best chance for developing the mutual strategic trust needed to move toward common ground on thornier issues. The following three pillars would seem the most sensible policy tools in undergirding such an approach:

Use the APEC and reciprocal Sunnylands summits to get the relationship back on track. Many Chinese strategic thinkers believe the summit marks a critical juncture for shaping the trajectory of bilateral ties in the remaining years of the Obama administration. This year's Strategic and Economic Dialogue failed to act as a policy springboard for paving the way for a successful summit. Instead, it released a relatively bland series of pronouncements that, after the summer in both capitals and an intense focus early in the fall on critical domestic events in each country, leaves precious little time to think about policy solutions for elevating the relationship. Along with progress on climate change and counterterrorism, the administration should seek to disarm Xi with an unexpected gesture of support, such as endorsing China's proposed Asian Infrastructure Investment Bank, or at least dropping our clumsy efforts to undermine it.

Put more energy into the Bilateral Investment Treaty (BIT) negotiations. President Xi and Premier Li Keqiang took a substantial domestic political risk in endorsing the BIT at last fall's watershed Third Plenum. The United States should more clearly articulate its appreciation of that gesture with greater activism while simultaneously pushing the Chinese negotiators to shift from aspirational enthusiasm for the treaty toward detailing real concessions the Chinese side is willing to make. The BIT also represents the best mechanism for the United States to affect the trajectory of China's economic reforms, which has critical implications for the more challenging business environment U.S. and other foreign firms currently are grappling with in China.

Get TPP done. The rebalance can have no credibility in the region without the TPP's successful conclusion, because the pact reflects the crystallization of the policy vis-à-vis China. It reassures U.S. allies and partners that they need not focus exclusively on the pull of China's economy while also providing a vehicle for those in China who acknowledge that, like China's World Trade Organization accession more than a decade ago, TPP may provide a more politically palatable pathway for making the difficult changes at home that Chinese leaders agree they must enact for their own prosperity.

Despite concerns about Washington's implementation of the rebalance, the United States is well positioned to lead in Asia. Decades of U.S. engagement have enabled Asia's economic growth, security, and the spread of shared values. Today many regional states look to China to drive economic growth, but they rely more than ever on the United States to guarantee regional security. For this reason, it is critical that regional allies, partners, and competitors recognize and acknowledge that the United States is a Pacific power with the ability to carry out its rebalance strategy.

Implementing the rebalance will require that the United States maintain its longstanding political relationships, robust economic ties, unparalleled military capabilities, and shared values with most regional states. Although the perception in Asia is that the United States and its rebalance to the region have lost some steam, 2015 provides an opportunity for Washington to demonstrate that U.S. engagement will not only continue, but will grow.

PART V

Is a Competing Economic Order Emerging?

25. THE EVOLVING INSTITUTIONAL LANDSCAPE

Matthew P. Goodman

Seventy years ago, as World War II was nearing its end, 44 allied nations assembled at the Bretton Woods resort in New Hampshire to begin rebuilding a global economic order that had been reduced to rubble over the previous 30 years. The institutions spawned by that meeting, including the International Monetary Fund (IMF), World Bank, and eventually World Trade Organization (WTO), underpinned a rules-based economic order that produced seven decades of growing prosperity around the world.

Over the past decade, the credibility of these multilateral institutions has been brought into question by two failings: frequent inability to deliver on their mandate, be it stronger growth or freer trade; and outdated governance structures that do not reflect the rise of China or the other emerging economies. Various efforts have been made to fix these problems, from IMF quota reform to WTO ministerial conferences, but most of these efforts have so far failed to deliver.

As a number of developments over the past year brought into sharp focus, some countries—including industrialized economies—are tired of waiting for existing institutions to perform better and have started to pursue workarounds. Some of these initiatives have been consciously designed to bolster and reenergize the multilateral order, while others appear to have been motivated by narrower considerations. But in either case, there is a risk that these new arrangements could damage the existing order if not structured and governed appropriately.

Trade is one area where workarounds are becoming the norm. Frustrated by a decade of unproductive multilateral negotiations under the Doha Development Agenda, Group of 20 (G20) leaders meeting in Cannes in November 2011 called for "fresh, credible approaches" to trade liberalization. This helped spur agreement at Bali in December 2013 on a new multilateral deal on trade facilitation, designed to lower border frictions to trade. Yet within months this agreement had unraveled, as India blocked final consensus.

Meanwhile, various groups of WTO members have been pursuing regional trade arrangements outside the Doha framework. In the Asia-Pacific region, talks are underway along two tracks, the Trans-Pacific Partnership (TPP) and the Regional Comprehensive Economic Partnership (RCEP). The United States and European Union are negotiating a Transatlantic Trade and Investment Partnership (TTIP). Although all of these negotiations have been slow going, there is a reasonable prospect that one or all of these mega-regional deals will be struck within the next two to three years.

Along with attempts to negotiate sectoral agreements such as an updated Information Technology Agreement (ITA-II) and a Trade in Services Agreement (TISA), these new plurilateral arrangements could be seen as a threat to the multilateral system. However, provided they remain open to new members and build on existing rules rather than undermining them, these workarounds could lay out an alternative path to a new "21st-century" set of trade rules, after years of failed attempts to reach the multilateral summit directly via the Doha round.

Meanwhile, attempts to reform the original Bretton Woods institutions to align their governance structures with the new global balance of economic power have made little progress. In 2010, the United States championed an agreement in the G20 to reallocate "shares and chairs" in the IMF from the advanced countries of Europe toward large emerging markets. But these reforms have stalled due to failure of the U.S. Congress to ratify an IMF capital increase that underpins the deal.

Emerging markets have clearly lost patience with the slow progress on institutional reform and have started to pursue their own workarounds. Meeting with Southeast Asian leaders in late 2013, Chinese President Xi Jinping proposed an Asian Infrastructure Investment Bank (AIIB) to help meet the region's enormous infrastructure needs, estimated at some $1 trillion per annum over the next decade. Then in July 2014, Brazil, Russia, India, China, and South Africa launched a New Development Bank—commonly known as the "BRICS Bank"—that would pool the group's resources to finance development projects in the five countries and possibly beyond.

While many details of the AIIB and BRICS Bank remain to be worked out, these initiatives clearly signal an impulse among their founders—and especially China—for more voice in global economic governance. The real question is whether these new institutions will enhance the rules-based order or detract from it. In an encouraging sign, Beijing has gone out of its way to clarify that the governance structure and operational practices of the AIIB, including environmental and other lending standards, will be transparent and consistent with the practices of the Asian Development Bank and other existing multilateral institutions.

Finally, what of the G20? Established as a leader-level forum in 2008, the G20 was effectively a reversal of an earlier workaround, the G7, which the advanced industrialized democracies had created in the 1970s initially to meet their needs as energy consumers. Expanding the table to include major emerging countries, the G20 generated unprecedented international economic cooperation to combat the global financial crisis at its first few summits. However, the forum has suffered in recent years from a waning sense of shared purpose and an inability to deliver visible results on its core mission of strong growth, financial stability, and international financial architecture reform. As host in 2014, Australia sought to restore the G20's credibility by seeking concrete outcomes under the themes "growth and resilience," but 2015 host Turkey is likely to have its work cut out in sustaining the G20's role as steering group for the global economy.

For all the questions about the effectiveness and legitimacy of existing multilateral institutions, and for all the recent efforts at workarounds, it is worth remembering that the postwar rules-based economic order has produced unprecedented prosperity over the past seven decades. It is difficult to believe that a fundamentally different set of institutions and rules could have produced better outcomes.

The big question going forward is whether key countries have the necessary combination of willingness and capability to reform and strengthen the existing order. The United States, Europe, and Japan still have the will, but their capacity has been diminished by slow growth, fiscal constraints, and political dysfunction. China, India, and other emerging economies have growing capabilities but have not yet consistently demonstrated a willingness to lead in this area. Thus fluidity is likely to remain the hallmark of global economic governance for the foreseeable future.

26. STRENGTHENING THE EXISTING ORDER

Amy Studdart

The pages of the economic press are not the place to look if you are feeling gloomy about the future of the liberal order: "Japan's corporate confidence fades," "Germany slashes its economic forecasts," "Yen tensions rise," "The euro zone: that sinking feeling (again)." Along with the United States, Japan and Europe represent the pillars of the Bretton Woods system, but unlike the United States, confidence in their economic prospects is low. It is understandable why emerging economies have been looking for alternatives: no matter how useful the tools and rules of Bretton Woods have proven to be, the economies that underpin it don't look hugely appealing.

Between them, Japan and Europe have five seats at the table of the G7. The BRICS have none. Within the International Monetary Fund (IMF) Europe has 35.6 percent of the voting power, Japan has 6.7 percent, and the BRICS share 11.5 percent. As seen from China, Brazil, India and other emerging economics, these numbers represent an outdated sense of economic power and reflect neither the emergence of new major economies nor the impact of the 2008 financial crisis. But Japan and the European Union continue to represent more than a third of global GDP and have historically been responsible stakeholders. Without them, Bretton Woods is a one-legged stool.

The predominant response of emerging countries to the shift in economic power over the last year has been to experiment with the establishment of new, alternative institutions, not so loosely based on the architecture of the old: the Asian Infrastructure Investment Bank (AIIB) and the BRICS bank mirror the functions of the Asian Development Bank (ADB), IMF, and World Bank; and BRICS summits are not dissimilar to the G7 format. While these institutions need not necessarily compete with their predecessors, the tendency toward creating alternatives, combined with protectionist instincts on trade, marks a worrying shift away from a mutually supportive, integrated global framework.

The similarities of these institutions to those that already exist reflect that there is much about the current order worth preserving. It is a rules-based system that has tended to reward multilateralism and international cooperation over the pursuit of a narrow conception of self-interest. Without it, it is unlikely that the emerging economies would have developed as quickly or as robustly as they have. But that order—unadjusted to new political and economic realities—is fraying as countries start to feel that working around the system will yield more benefits than working within it. The creation of more inclusive institutions like the G20 has not been enough to stop the process.

If the global economic order is to persist, Europe and Japan will need to help create an environment in which emerging economies are incentivized to become stakeholders within the existing system rather than to create a new one. This will require the promise of economic dynamism and strong political leadership that can negotiate adjustments to the system that better reflect today's balance of power without compromising on the need for responsibility. While reporting on frameworks like the BRICS has tended to focus on the geopolitical, the world's emerging economies are primarily looking for new sources of growth. Over the last few years, they have largely seen that momentum and opportunity in one another, and especially in China.

But while the developing world has been seen as the driving force behind the global economy over the last decade and a half, growth rates are slowing. In July, the IMF's World Economic Outlook revised their prediction for this year's global growth down by 0.3 percent, citing "a less optimistic outlook for several emerging markets." China's promised economic reforms have progressed in fits and starts, and even the success of that plan would see a diminished demand for the resource exports that have driven the growth of countries like Brazil. The IMF predicts that the growth rate of advanced economies will see an uptick between 2014 (1.8 percent) and 2015 (2.4 percent). In contrast, China's growth is predicted to fall from 7.7 percent in 2014 to 6.8 percent in 2015.

The net result is that Japan, Europe, and, in turn, the Bretton Woods system of global economic governance could again start to look more appealing. In Japan, this will rest on proving that the initial bout of confidence in Abenomics—Prime Minister Abe's plan to revitalize the Japanese economy—is not misplaced. For the European Union, it will require a unified economic plan and strong enough political leadership to see that plan through. Given the recent figures on real wage depreciation in Japan and downward revisions for Germany's economic growth, this is a tall order.

When the U.S.-Europe-Japan Trialogue was established in 1973, the statement of purpose said that the three sides "bear a special responsibility for developing effective cooperation, both in their own interests and in those of the rest of the world. They share a number of problems which, if not solved, could cause difficulty for all." There have been few instances where that has been truer than now. The problem with the global economic order is not that the institutions are irrelevant, but instead that two of the pillars that support it look like they are crumbling. Will a new global economic order emerge? Maybe. But if Europe and Japan get their economies on the right track, it is far more likely that the existing order will simply adapt.

27. THE EVOLUTION OF THE GLOBAL TRADING SYSTEM

Scott Miller

Five years ago, Moises Naim observed in *Foreign Policy* that the need for effective multicountry collaboration had been rising steadily since the 1990s but attempts to craft multilateral agreements had consistently failed. "Minilateralism," the notion of conducting international governance by assembling the fewest parties necessary for the largest effect, was Naim's alternative in light of the repeated failure of "big" multiparty deals. The trading system faces just such a challenge today.

The General Agreement on Trade and Tariffs (GATT) 1994 was one of the last "big" multiparty deals. Twenty years on, the World Trade Organization (WTO) members have not once reached agreement to amend the structure on a multilateral basis. Even a small, universally beneficial agreement on trade facilitation—announced with great fanfare in December 2013—unraveled this summer when it came time to implement the deal. And never mind the Doha Development Agenda (DDA), launched in 2001 and scheduled to conclude in three years, which hangs around like a snoring party guest, obstructing discussion on other issues as the memory of its onetime relevance fades.

Thanks to the "win-win" character of voluntary exchange, trade goes on and traders muddle through. Total merchandise trade achieved a record-high $17.3 trillion in 2012, growing at an average annual rate of 9 percent since the launch of the DDA in 2001. The trading system works reasonably well, due in part to the strong core disciplines of the GATT, especially the principle of nondiscrimination and the obligation of members to act in the "least trade restrictive" manner. Additionally, GATT 1994's Dispute Settlement Understanding continues to command respect among the parties and helps to avoid policy drift. Traders appreciate the rules and live with the problems and inconsistencies. In truth, trade would flourish even in the absence of trade rules. Consider hydrocarbons, which amount to 18 percent of world merchandise trade despite there being practically no agreed disciplines. Likewise, millions of people around the world have seen their diet improved over the past 20 years thanks to growing trade in agricultural products, despite persistent protectionist measures.

TECHNOLOGY LEADS THE WAY
The WTO may be stuck, but trade policy has by no means stood still. Regional economic cooperation—in the form of regional trading arrangements (RTAs) or bilateral/regional free trade agreements (FTAs)—has been the political "path of least resistance." Over 200 RTAs have been concluded and operate in concert with treaty-based protection for foreign investors, creating a network for efficient commerce. The rise in RTAs occurred in parallel to dramatic changes in information, communication, and transportation technology often referred to as "globalization." Technological progress caused barriers to the movement of goods, services, people, ideas, and culture to fall; lowered barriers led to further innovation in the way products are designed, produced, and marketed. RTAs were a logical policy response to technological progress.

Even as technological change widens the gap between commercial realities and trade policy, sophisticated RTA negotiators are discovering solutions to new issues. Electronic commerce is an example. There was no commercial use of the Internet in 1994 when the most recent GATT agreement entered into force. Subsequent FTAs negotiated by the United States have steadily improved rules and practices, and today's negotiators continue to refine and extend the disciplines. In the absence of a broad multilateral framework, RTAs have provided a vital outlet to develop international trade architecture (and innovations therein).

NOTHING SUCCEEDS LIKE SUCCESS

Why is international trade architecture evolving "bottom-up," through RTAs instead of a multilateral agreement? Principally because of a split among the big traders. Trade policy views are divided between advanced industrial economies that support trade liberalization and large emerging economies that favor a larger role for state intervention. This split has been evident in the Doha talks since negotiations collapsed in July 2008. Disagreement about the liberal trade regime will not be easily overcome, since state capitalism offers stability over growth, while allowing governments to capture rents. This basic divide exists not just among WTO members, but also in the G20 and other arrangements.

Over time, trade agreements that offer practical benefits tend to grow, in both members and the range of disciplines. GATT rules solved important problems in constructive ways, and the agreement's membership grew from 102 economies in 1986 to 160 today. The Trans-Pacific Partnership (TPP) was conceived as a way to modernize and raise standards for trade and investment among a dozen diverse Pacific Rim economies with existing RTAs. If negotiators succeed in crafting broadly acceptable, neutral rules for issues like digital commerce, state-owned enterprises, or localization requirements, others outside of the talks may adopt the provisions, whether by joining TPP or incorporating similar disciplines in another agreement. Net, TPP could become the "next big thing" on grounds of utility. In any case, a new trade architecture is more likely to emerge in an organic, bottom-up fashion than as a colossal production of a big multilateral conference.

28. GEOPOLITICAL INSTABILITY AND ENERGY MARKETS

Sarah Ladislaw

The foreign policy world is churning about the current state of global affairs, leading some to argue that we are witnessing an era of major realignment in global power structures. If this is true, regional powers will see an opening to strike a new balance, seek incremental gains, settle old scores, and improve their standing. This leaves energy sectors particularly vulnerable.

The geopolitical landscape and energy often impact one another. Geopolitical turmoil can affect energy markets and energy trends can upset geopolitical dynamics. In the first instance, political risk and instability affect the vitality of local, regional, and sometimes even global energy markets by causing supply disruptions or stymying investment. Recent examples of this include supply outages and under investment in Libya, Nigeria, and Venezuela among others. In the second instance, large resource discoveries can alter internal domestic or regional tensions or perceptions of relationships. The most prominent current example of this is the surge of shale gas and light tight oil in the United States and the perception of geopolitical realignment and leverage this energy market development brings. This symbiotic relationship between energy and geopolitics has been true in many parts of the world since the beginning of the modern energy economy.

What then might an age of geopolitical realignment mean for energy? The conventional wisdom thus far is that we are living in an era of heightened above-ground risk for energy investors. Oddly enough, however, at least in the realm of global oil markets, heightened geopolitical risk in some of the world's largest energy producers has not led to a dramatic increase in oil prices. Part of the rationale is that market fundamentals are weak, there is adequate supply despite record outages, and demand looks soft. Moreover, even in areas where there is definite political strife, major oil and gas supplies are not necessarily at direct risk.

Lack of a near-term price response does not necessarily mean a lack of risk or impact, however. Energy is often used as a tool in many geopolitical struggles. It is targeted for tactical and strategic aims in conflict areas—recent examples include the fights over oil fields, pipelines, refineries, and export terminals in places like Libya, Northern Iraq, and Nigeria. It is used as a tool for messaging intent and asserting authority, like the recent deployment of a drilling rig into contested South China Sea waters as a "mobile manifestation of Chinese sovereignty." Energy is used as a point of leverage, a negotiation tool, and, indeed, a weapon. This has only become more pervasive in the age of economic statecraft. No longer is "energy leverage" only about Russia seeking to constrain European foreign and domestic policy through the use of its leverage as natural gas supplier, but it is also about a coalition of governments using a variety of sanctions to restrict investment in future oil production in Russia as part of a broader strategy to bring about a course correction to Russia's current posture toward Ukraine.

While none of these discrete activities are particularly new, the culmination of them makes so-called "above-ground issues" matter more to the energy sector than ever before. An age of realignment and heightened geopolitical tension when the energy sector is already experiencing disruptive change on a variety of levels—from unconventional oil and gas development, the declining cost of solar, decentralization and digitization of energy systems, slow and uneven growth, and rising investment costs—could dampen or accelerate investments by location. During periods like this, some countries will seek to shore up energy trade flows through the erection of new trade deals or by making infrastructure investments that tie countries together. Other countries and companies will start to question the costs and benefits of being tied to the international financial system and start to explore the feasibility and limitations of alternative systems and arrangements to underpin their energy investments. And nearly everyone, from private companies to state-owned enterprises and sovereign governments will reevaluate the political risk exposure in their portfolio and their approach to managing resource development. 2015 promises to be both an uncertain and opportunistic time.

29. DIVERGENT PERSPECTIVES OF THE DEMOCRATIC BRICS

A Conversation with Carl Meacham, Jennifer G. Cooke, and Richard M. Rossow moderated by Amy Studdart

The BRICS grouping has emerged over the last year as one of the most significant gatherings of economic power in the world. No longer just a talk shop, the most recent summit in Brazil saw the creation of the BRICS Bank, the first concrete institution formalizing future cooperation. The success of the grouping has been surprising. The BRICS members have fundamentally different economies, politics, and, presumably, reasons for wanting to be associated with the BRICS framework. Arguably, the three democracies in the group--Brazil, India, and South Africa--share more with the West in terms of political systems and values than they do with China and Russia. In the interview that follows, CSIS experts tease out the reasons why the BRICS framework has been so successful in those three countries.

Carl Meacham, director of the Americas program talks about Brazil's approach; Jennifer Cooke, director of the Africa program, addresses South Africa's role; and Rick Rossow, director of the India program, explains what the BRICS has meant to India in the past, and how that might change under a new government.

Amy Studdart: What is the significance of being a part of the BRICS to Brazil, India, and South Africa?

Carl Meacham: In many ways what the BRICS countries share is their individual incomparability. Within its own regional or subregional context, each BRICS member clearly stands out. But unlike its fellow BRICS, Brazil is not an undisputed leader in its region—a region it shares with the United States. But it is the largest, most promising, and fastest-growing developing country in the Western Hemisphere, and that isn't to be taken lightly. In a region accustomed to U.S. leadership and dominance, Brazil is a rising star—and one that increasingly demands to be taken seriously on its own terms.

Richard M. Rossow: For India, creating the BRICS as an alternative to the Bretton Woods institutions made sense when the Congress Party was leading the country. Congress' commitment to "nonalignment," while perhaps a bit weaker than when Jawaharlal Nehru was prime minister, remains an overriding principle of the Party's foreign policy. They prefer to spread their chips across the table, instead of placing heavy bets on any individual partnerships. Supporting alternative development institutions made sense.

So far the Modi government's foreign policy is a mix of shoring up relations with immediate neighbors, and courting larger countries to make critical investments into India. The support for the creation of the BRICS institutions in July 2014 does not appear aligned with the primary objectives of the Modi government's overall foreign policy. It remains to be seen if the July summit was merely following through prior commitments while the government carved out its own foreign policy goals, or if support for BRICS remains strong. Prime Minister Modi's own statements on the need for BRICS refer to weakness in major economies, the need for people-to-people exchanges, and a concern about the impact of developed nation's monetary policy on the Indian market.

Jennifer G. Cooke: South Africa is an odd choice for inclusion in the BRICS grouping. The country's infrastructure and financial service base are relatively sophisticated compared to much of Africa, but with a GDP of just $351 billion in 2013 and a population of 50 million, it is not exactly poised to become a driver of global economic growth. Nigeria, with a bigger and faster-growing economy and triple South Africa's population would arguably have been a better African candidate. But being the grouping's sole African member may give South Africa a boost in global prestige, burnish its credential as a representative of "African" interests in global forums (a notion that other African countries might dispute), and perhaps most important, afford it greater and more frequent access to investment and borrowing opportunities with Chinese and Indian counterparts. It also fits with a popular ideological rhetoric within segments of the ruling African National Congress of a South Africa that stands up to the overweening influence of Western powers.

Studdart: How do India, Brazil, and South Africa view their relationship with China within the BRICS framework?

Rossow: It has been surprising to see the Narendra Modi-led BJP government maintain the nation's support for the BRICS institutions. The BJP [Bharatiya Janata Party) leans more toward a "realpolitik" foreign policy, and views China as the country's long-term strategic and economic competitor. While aligning with China on BRICS activities provides some important positive connectivity, it is difficult to envision India playing anything but a junior role in this "partnership," which will create pressure in New Delhi to withdraw.

Meacham: China is, at this point, pivotal to the Brazilian economy—and it is this economic closeness that forms the lion's share of the Brazil-China relationship. China is, without a doubt, a strategic partner for Brazil in economic terms, though the two countries differ on many fundamental issues. But those issues aside, China is Brazil's largest trading partner. Trade flows have grown over tenfold since 2003, making the two the biggest partners within the BRICS. Brazil is among China's largest destinations for foreign direct investment, with Chinese cash fueling construction and development projects across Brazil. So, in short, Brazil's relationship with China—both within the BRICS and outside that framework—is fundamentally an economic one focused on the two countries' overlapping interests and growth trajectories.

Cooke: Views within South Africa about its burgeoning relationship with China are mixed. The South African leadership has been very open to partnership with the Chinese, and President Zuma has assiduously cultivated the diplomatic and commercial relationship, which plays well within nationalist, far-left factions of the ANC [African National Congress]. But the whole-hearted embrace of China has not been without controversy, with some critics arguing that in its rush to find alternatives to traditional Western partners, South Africa risks becoming overly beholden to a new great power. The Dalai Lama has been refused an entry visa into South Africa three times in the last three years (once after receiving a personal invitation to celebrate the birthday of anti-apartheid hero Bishop Desmond Tutu), leading some critics to paint Zuma as a new lackey of the Chinese. The import of inexpensive Chinese goods, particularly textiles and clothing, has hit local manufacturers and the textile industry hard. And President Zuma himself voiced concern over the lopsided nature of the relationship, calling the supply of raw materials to China without benefit of local value addition unsustainable.

Studdart: Each of the BRICS countries is also a member of the G20. What do South Africa, India, and Brazil hope to achieve through the BRICS framework that they cannot through the G20?

Cooke: Aside from an occasional rhetorical flourish, South Africa under President Jacob Zuma has not shown much real interest in trying to reshape the global rules through the G20 or any other global forum. For the most part, BRIC membership is seen less as a vehicle to advance a global strategic vision than as a means to advancing South Africa's national commercial and economic interests. Membership in the smaller group gives South Africa greater global cachet, and a more exclusive relationship with China. In time, however, and with more focused intention, South African leadership may calculate that it will have greater influence in a smaller, South-South grouping than the more diffuse G20, and that the grouping could potentially serve as a vanguard for a broader constituency for global governance reform.

Rossow: India shows habitual concern about the development of global economic pacts and standards where it does not exhibit sufficient influence alone. The World Trade Organization is the most obvious example, but India has voiced concerns about developments in other areas such as Internet governance, global taxation regulation, patents, and more.

Meacham: In many ways, the flexible BRICS format is the best-case scenario for Brazilian engagement in the world, given the country's preference for nonbinding interactions on the global stage. The summit-style arrangement and its inherent malleability are what make the forum so appealing to Brazil. Through the summits, Brazil is empowered to identify those areas in which cooperation would best suit its own needs. In many ways, Brazil's engagement with the BRICS reflects Brazil's increasing tendency to look to the global economy to address its own development goals. The BRICS framework complements Brazil's more established partnerships in innovation and research, providing a low-risk but potentially high-reward alternative to the existing order.

The BRICS summit in Brazil this summer demonstrated an as-yet unseen coordination among the member states for the future of the alliance—a future that probably could extend beyond complementing the present world order. But it would likely be difficult to align the objectives of the five members on a broad range of economic, geopolitical, and security issues, given their asymmetrical interests.

PART VI

Will Ebola Evolve from a Health Crisis to an Economic and Governance Crisis?

30. THE TRAJECTORY OF EBOLA AND OUR RESPONSE

J. Stephen Morrison

Ebola in West Africa is a modern plague, unlike anything we have seen. In less than a year since the epidemic reportedly began, President Obama, the UN Security Council, World Health Organization (WHO) Director General Margaret Chan, and others have declared the epidemic a grave threat to security in Africa and beyond—including the United States. By late October, there were 10,000 confirmed cases, and over 5,000 deaths in Guinea, Liberia, and Sierra Leone. (The largest previous outbreak, in Gulu, northern Uganda, in 2000, was 424 cases.) These numbers, thought to represent as little as a quarter of the true scale, are expanding exponentially, doubling every 20 days. By early December, the epidemic is expected to reach 10,000 new cases per week.

The precise trajectory in 2015 is difficult to predict, as West Africa heads into the unknown. Under a worst-case scenario laid out by the U.S. Centers for Disease Control and Prevention (CDC), the total number of cases in Liberia and Sierra Leone could reach 1.4 million in January 2015. Under less extreme projections that assume quicker international progress in bringing the epidemic under control, the number might be half, a quarter, or less, but none of these options is comforting. Whichever scenario materializes, it is safe to expect that the epidemic will march forward at a fierce pace into 2015. That will happen in parallel with an international mobilization, led by the United States, the United Kingdom, and the UN Mission for Ebola Emergency Response (UNMEER), that races against time—incrementally—to put in place structures and programs that, it is hoped, will cut the chain of transmission across countless communities. The backdrop will feature steady economic regression, worsening food insecurity, and health systems in collapse that leave people without access to safe delivery, malaria treatment and control programs, and care for diabetes, along with other critical services.

For U.S. policymakers, Ebola is a tricky two-front war, fought both at home and abroad. It is now the task before Ron Klain, the newly appointed White House Ebola coordinator (czar) to figure out the way forward.

In an unprecedented military-led international health intervention, President Obama pledged in September the deployment of U.S. forces (now upwards of 4,000) and $1 billion over the first six months. ($750 million in military assistance has been committed, with the option of another $250 million. U.S. civilian emergency assistance exceeds $350 million.)

At home, all visitors arriving from Sierra Leone, Liberia, and Guinea are now routed through five hub airports where they are subject to advanced screenings. The U.S. military has assembled a 30-person emergency medical team and CDC has begun to deploy "swat teams," each to assist hospitals across the country that find themselves handling Ebola cases, before those cases are transferred to one of four biocontainment facilities. CDC protocols for the handling of Ebola cases have been revised and strengthened, and training of medical personnel has intensified across the nation.

Ebola's two fronts are interdependent and at times in considerable tension with one another.

It is not possible to reduce the threat of importation of Ebola into the United States if the source—burgeoning Ebola in West Africa—is not quickly brought under control, if not extinguished altogether. Yet how, when, and if control of Ebola in West Africa is to be achieved remain highly uncertain propositions. And the longer these uncertainties persist, the more difficult it will become to sustain essential political and financial commitments by the White House and Congress to stay the course in West Africa, and the more difficult it will become to fend off an increasingly frightened population in the United States that demands greater unilateral protections at our points of entry. These crosscutting pressures will only intensify. As the initial first six months draws to a close in the first quarter of 2015, the Obama administration, Congress, the media, and the American people will debate difficult, messy choices.

At home on American soil, the overriding goal is to protect Americans, minimize the importation of cases, and when cases do appear, ensure U.S. health institutions are equipped to contain outbreaks. It is fundamentally a battle to manage fear, preserve confidence, strengthen capacities to control infection and trace contacts, and thereby minimize the threat that the disease poses to individuals, to front-line institutions like Texas Health Presbyterian Hospital, and to the credibility of the presidency itself (including the reform of U.S. health system under the Affordable Care Act) and key public health agencies like the CDC. As we discovered following the Liberian Thomas Eric Duncan's arrival in Dallas in September, and the subsequent secondary infections of the two nurses, a very few bungled cases can swiftly ignite public panic, recriminations, and a political emergency that reaches into the White House. At the same time these incidents raise pressures for a travel ban and the tightening of visas, steps that reach beyond enhanced thermal screening and interviews at major U.S. airport hubs. If harsh exclusionary measures are imposed, however, these could weaken commercial air links and the flow of essential health workers, emergency personnel, and commodities. That in turn will worsen pressures upon the U.S. military to fill the resulting gaps and aggravate the perception within West Africa that medieval quarantine measures are being imposed.

In Liberia, the overriding U.S. goal is to cut the chain of transmission by effectively isolating those who have been exposed
and infected from all others. That is a tall order that requires
the rapid entry of a flood of personnel and goods. The vital
U.S. military contributions in Liberia are to create a command-
and-control capacity; erect an air bridge from Dakar, Senegal;
construct a health worker training center, a 25-bed facility for
care of health workers, and 17 treatment facilities with 1,700
beds; and deliver mobile laboratories, protective gear for health
workers, and thousands of home care kits. The operational delivery of emergency health services is the responsibility of some
combination of nongovernmental groups and civilian contrac-
tors, though how exactly that interface is to be managed has yet
to be sorted out.

There are not yet answers to several other fundamental questions. Across the three countries, upwards of 20,000 trained
national and international staff are required, at least half in
Liberia, yet recruitment continues to be seriously impeded by
the highly lethal threat of Ebola itself, a worsening climate of
instability and chaos, and uncertainty about whether international staff will be guaranteed adequate health care, including
medevac arrangements to Europe or North America. For the
United States and others to be confident that both the threat of
Ebola across the region will be addressed effectively, and that a
future handoff to a multilateral effort will be possible, it is critical that other major donors come soon to the table with major
commitments and begin to deliver quickly, especially in neighboring Sierra Leone and Guinea. Filling out the donor ranks
and spurring quick action, however, remain problematic. There
has been recent progress. The United Kingdom has committed
750 troops and 300 million pounds; the World Bank and IMF
over $400 million in emergency facilities; and the EU 130 mil-
lion euros. The Chinese have pledged $200 million, including
200 medical personnel, and the Cubans over 400 doctors and
other skilled medical staff. Interestingly, Mark Zuckerberg, Bill
Gates, and Paul Allen have stepped forward with, respectively,

$25, $50, and $126 million in quick-disbursing assistance to fill critical gaps. But despite these gains, the shortfall in pledges for UNMEER's $988 million appeal is over $630 million. Given the uncertainty, fear, and risk, many donors are hanging back.

The stability of Liberia, Sierra Leone, and Guinea remains an open question: the danger is real that current governing structures, being weak, corrupt, and widely held in popular contempt, could dissolve into violent chaos. There has been discussion of the possibility of the Ebola virus mutating to become airborne, and of terrorists using Ebola as a bioweapon: both possibilities are remote but do incite fear in the blogosphere and elsewhere. Far more plausible is the risk that Ebola will become endemic to the large coastal cities where it is now rampant, and that it will spread to other neighboring states. Most vulnerable are Ivory Coast, Ghana, and Mali. While Senegal and Nigeria have scored early successes in managing Ebola cases, each remains vulnerable.

There is awareness of the acute need to accelerate the development of new technology tools—vaccines, therapies, rapid tests—and much action is under way in each area. Realistically, progress will be slow. There is reason to be hopeful, but new solutions are not expected to become widely available for some time, and are not expected to shape outcomes in this current urgent phase.

Debate over post–Ebola reconstruction has not yet begun, but will become increasingly important. The same is true for what the international community should do to repair a broken WHO that failed at critical moments in 2014 to intervene and sound the alarm, despite prodding from Doctors Without Borders (MSF), the true heroes of this tragic saga, and other witnesses.

In closing, U.S. leadership in response to the Ebola crisis has been bold, ambitious, risky, and quickly evolving. It rests on unprecedented military commitments to answer a dangerous modern plague. It tests our nation's resolve on two complex fronts that will remain in tension with one another. It requires navigating profound uncertainties.

31. THE ECONOMIC IMPACT OF THE EBOLA OUTBREAK

Daniel F. Runde and Conor M. Savoy

Ebola is quickly moving from a regional public health crisis to a regional economic and political crisis that threatens to overwhelm the fragile development gains made by Sierra Leone and Liberia over the past decade.

Beyond the immediate impact the disease is having on the public health systems of the three countries affected, Ebola is now having a significant economic impact. At the moment this is confined primarily to the tri-country region of Liberia, Sierra Leone, and Guinea, but as borders remain closed, there is a growing possibility that it could threaten the broader West African region's economic well-being.

The World Bank estimates that in the short term, meaning for the remainder of the year, Guinea will see a reduction in GDP of 2.1 percent, Liberia will see a reduction of 3.4 percent, and Sierra Leone's GDP will be reduced by 3.3 percent. Moreover, the fiscal impact for each country is significant, with Liberia seeing a loss of $93 million, Sierra Leone $79 million, and Guinea $120 million.

Each of these numbers is significant on its own. What makes the numbers truly startling is that these states are some of the poorest on the poorest continent in the world. Liberia and Sierra Leone are both slowly recovering from disastrous civil wars that were only resolved in the early 2000s. Since then, both have seen significant economic gains. This has included high GDP growth rates that have helped to generate additional revenues to help fund critical investments. In addition, both have attracted impressive amounts of foreign direct investment (FDI), with Liberia alone seeing $16 billion in FDI since the end of the civil war. These trends are now in danger of being reversed.

On a country level, Ebola is causing commerce to grind to halt. Some of the hardest-hit areas in the tri-country area are the "bread basket" regions and this, combined with the closing of national borders, is causing food prices to spike. This has already caused citizens to horde food, but the worst may be to come if prices continue to rise and may trigger civilian unrest. Liberia's economy, for example, is dominated by mining, agriculture, and services, all of which are coming under severe strain. China Union, one of two iron ore producers in Liberia, suspended operations at its facilities in Liberia in August. ArcelorMittal, the other iron ore producer, is suspending its expansion plans. On the agricultural side, palm oil and rubber producers are reducing production, which has significant implications for export earners.

International financial institutions such as the International Monetary Fund, World Bank, and African Development Bank have responded with significant support packages for the three countries. In addition, several bilateral donors, including the United States, have pledged financial and material support to help the countries control and stabilize the outbreak. These all represent good short-term support that should help Liberia, Guinea, and Sierra Leone bare the initial costs of this crisis. To be sure, the international community needs to focus on stopping the spread of Ebola, but planning should also begin for helping these countries to recover rapidly once the disease is under control and the crisis passes.

What seems clear from the cases of Liberia and Sierra Leone is how quickly the institutions of state are being overwhelmed by Ebola. The most obvious manifestation of this is the local public health services, which were weak prior to the Ebola outbreak. The danger now is that as the outbreak continues, other government institutions will begin to be affected by the disease. If this happens, then recovery from this crisis will be far more difficult.

The Ebola crisis in West Africa is, unfortunately, a stark reminder that for all of the "Africa rising" stories there are significant challenges remaining at the country level. Liberia and Sierra Leone have been two countries that many have sought to highlight as leading performers on the continent, in spite of their ongoing fragility. And, yet, it appears that these gains were relatively narrow and, as is so often the case, a major crisis is exposing a lack of resilience in existing institutions. The challenge for the governments of these three countries and international donors is to concentrate on building resilient institutional capacity that will help to guarantee that future economic gains are not lost to disease or other crises.

INDEX

A

Abenomics, 100

ADB. *See* Asian Development Bank

Afghan war, U.S. spending on, 61

African Development Bank, response to Ebola crisis, 120

African National Congress, 109, 110

AIIB. *See* Asian Infrastructure Investment Bank

Algeria
GDP per capita in, 64
per capita oil wealth in, 64
urbanization in, 63

Allen, Paul, and mobilization against Ebola, 117–118

al Qaeda. *See also* Jabhat al-Nusra
empowerment of, by use of military force against, 71
near enemy targets of, 61
violence perpetrated by (2013), 61

al Shabaab, violence perpetrated by (2013), 61

ANC. *See* African National Congress

APEC. *See* Asia-Pacific Economic Cooperation (APEC) summit

ArcelorMittal, response to Ebola crisis, 120

Armenia
association agreement with EU, 36–37
and Eurasian Economic Union, 37
Russian forces in, 52

Russian influence in, 36

ASEAN. *See* Association of Southeast Asian Nations (ASEAN)

Asia
elites in, confidence in U.S. leadership, 75
gray zone conflicts in, 8, 87
regional security of, 86
security of, economics and, 79–82
U.S. deterrence in, 7, 8, 9
U.S. "rebalance" to, 79
Asian perceptions of, 74–75, 81–82
China and, 89–91
India's view on, 83
Japan and, 86–88
presidential leadership of, 81

Asian Development Bank, 96, 99

Asian Infrastructure Investment Bank, 81, 90, 96, 99

Asia-Pacific Economic Cooperation (APEC) summit, 75, 89–90

Association of Southeast Asian Nations (ASEAN)
geopolitical importance of, 80
Treaty of Amity and Cooperation, 80
views on China, 80–81

Azerbaijan, Russian influence in, 37–38

CONTRIBUTORS

JON B. ALTERMAN is a senior vice president, holds the Zbigniew Brzezinski Chair in Global Security and Geostrategy, and is director of the Middle East Program at CSIS.

SAMUEL J. BRANNEN is a former senior fellow in the International Security Program at CSIS.

ERNEST Z. BOWER is a senior adviser, Sumitro Chair for Southeast Asia Studies, and codirector of the Pacific Partners Initiative at CSIS.

VICTOR CHA is a senior adviser and Korea Chair at CSIS and is a professor of government and director for Asian Studies at Georgetown University.

EDWARD C. CHOW is a senior fellow in the Energy and National Security Program at CSIS.

CRAIG COHEN is executive vice president at CSIS.

HEATHER A. CONLEY is senior vice president for Europe, Eurasia, and the Arctic and director of the Europe Program at CSIS.

JENNIFER G. COOKE is director of the Africa Program at CSIS.

ZACK COOPER is a fellow with the Japan Chair at CSIS, where he focuses on Asian security issues.

ANTHONY H. CORDESMAN holds the Arleigh A. Burke Chair in Strategy at CSIS.

JOSIANE GABEL is vice president for programs and institutional partnerships at CSIS.

MATTHEW P. GOODMAN holds the William E. Simon Chair in Political Economy at CSIS.

MICHAEL J. GREEN is senior vice president for Asia and Japan Chair at CSIS and an associate professor at the Edmund A. Walsh School of Foreign Service at Georgetown University.

JOHN J. HAMRE is president and CEO, Pritzker Chair, and director of the Brzezinski Institute at CSIS.

KATHLEEN H. HICKS is senior vice president, Henry A. Kissinger chair, and director of the International Security Program at CSIS.

CHRISTOHPER K. JOHNSON is a senior adviser and holds the Freeman Chair in China Studies at CSIS.

STEPHANIE SANOK KOSTRO is acting director of the CSIS Homeland Security and Counterterrorism Program and a senior fellow with the CSIS International Security Program.

ANDREW C. KUCHINS is a senior fellow and director of the Russia and Eurasia Program at CSIS.

SARAH O. LADISLAW is a senior fellow and director of the CSIS Energy and National Security Program.

MAREN LEED is senior adviser with the Harold Brown Chair in Defense Policy Studies at CSIS.

JAMES A. LEWIS is a senior fellow and director of the Strategic Technologies Program at CSIS.

HAIM MALKA is deputy director and senior fellow in the Middle East Program at CSIS.

JEFFREY MANKOFF is deputy director and fellow with the CSIS Russia and Eurasia Program.

CARL MEACHAM is director of the CSIS Americas Program.

SARAH E. MENDELSON is a senior adviser and director of the Human Rights Initiative at CSIS.

ANDREW A. MICHTA is an adjunct fellow with the CSIS Europe Program and the M.W. Buckman Distinguished Professor of International Studies at Rhodes College.

SCOTT MILLER is a senior adviser and holds the William M. Scholl Chair in International Business at CSIS.

J. STEPHEN MORRISON is senior vice president at CSIS and director of its Global Health Policy Center.

CLARK A. MURDOCK is a senior adviser for the U.S. Defense and National Security Group at CSIS and director of the Project on Nuclear Issues.

RICHARD M. ROSSOW is a senior fellow and holds the Wadhwani Chair in U.S.-India Policy Studies at CSIS.

DANIEL F. RUNDE is director of the Project on Prosperity and Development, holds the William A. Schreyer Chair in Global Analysis, and codirects the Project on U.S. Leadership in Development at CSIS.

THOMAS SANDERSON is codirector and senior fellow with the Transnational Threats Project at CSIS.

CONOR M. SAVOY is deputy director and fellow with the Project on U.S. Leadership in Development at CSIS.

SHARON SQUASSONI is director and senior fellow with the Proliferation Prevention Program at CSIS.

AMY STUDDART is deputy director and fellow of the William E. Simon Chair in Political Economy at CSIS.

NICHOLAS SZECHENYI is a senior fellow and deputy director of the Japan Chair at CSIS.

JUAN C. ZARATE is a senior adviser to the Transnational Threats Project and the Homeland Security and Counterterrorism Program at CSIS.

ABOUT CSIS

For over 50 years, the Center for Strategic and International Studies (CSIS) has worked to develop solutions to the world's greatest policy challenges. Today, CSIS scholars are providing strategic insights and bipartisan policy solutions to help decisionmakers chart a course toward a better world.

CSIS is a nonprofit organization headquartered in Washington, D.C. The Center's 220 full-time staff and large network of affiliated scholars conduct research and analysis and develop policy initiatives that look into the future and anticipate change.

Founded at the height of the Cold War by David M. Abshire and Admiral Arleigh Burke, CSIS was dedicated to finding ways to sustain American prominence and prosperity as a force for good in the world. Since 1962, CSIS has become one of the world's preeminent international institutions focused on defense and security; regional stability; and transnational challenges ranging from energy and climate to global health and economic integration.

Former U.S. senator Sam Nunn has chaired the CSIS Board of Trustees since 1999. Former deputy secretary of defense John J. Hamre became the Center's president and chief executive officer in 2000.

www.ingramcontent.com/pod-product-compliance
Lightning Source LLC
Chambersburg PA
CBHW050530270326
41926CB00015B/3151